Room at the Top
A DIY Guide to Loft Conversions

Other books by Robert Tattersall

Home Heating and Fireplaces
A DIY Guide

Robert Tattersall

Room at the Top

A DIY Guide to Loft Conversions

Stanley Paul
London Melbourne Sydney Auckland Johannesburg

Stanley Paul & Co. Ltd

An imprint of the Hutchinson Publishing Group

17–21 Conway Street, London W1P 5HL

Hutchinson Group (Australia) Pty Ltd
30–32 Cremorne Street, Richmond South, Victoria 3121
PO Box 151, Broadway, New South Wales 2007

Hutchinson Group (NZ) Ltd
32–34 View Road, PO Box 40-086, Glenfield, Auckland 10

Hutchinson Group (SA) (Pty) Ltd
PO Box 337, Bergvlei 2012, South Africa

First published 1982
© Robert Tattersall 1982

Set in Times by Computape (Pickering) Ltd,
Pickering, North Yorkshire

Printed in Great Britain by The Anchor Press Ltd,
and bound by Wm Brendon & Son Ltd,
both of Tiptree, Essex

ISBN 0 09 146851 5

Contents

Introduction

Moving house to a bigger and better place can be an expensive business. So you feel the need to spread yourself a little, to give a growing family extra bedroom space, provide separate quarters for an elderly relative who has come to live with you, perhaps set up a hobby room for adults, or a play-study den for children, even provide a nicer bathroom and kitchen, too? How much is all that going to cost you? It's not just a question of the difference in price between the house you now own and the bigger one you would like to have. There are also legal and estate agents' fees, the actual cost of the move and the price of the new curtains and floorcoverings you will need. It's enough to make anyone decide to stay put. But don't worry. You don't have to put up with a cramped form of lifestyle. It is possible to get that bigger house without being involved in an impossibly large spending spree. How? Simple! Enlarge the one you already have. It will cost you much less than buying another home, will save you legal and agent's fees, spare you the expense of moving, and the cost of providing floorcoverings, and curtains, etc., and involve much less upheaval in your family life. Moreover you can bring the cost down even further by tackling much of the work yourself. It is the aim of this book to describe one of the best forms of home extension – a room, or rooms, in the loft. It describes what is involved, tells you where you must seek expert help, what you must leave to a builder, and what you can do on a do-it-yourself basis. How much, in fact, you can do yourself depends on your skills, energies, courage and inclinations. But whatever you decide this book will, I hope, be of invaluable assistance.

1
The Planning

The attic occupies a specially emotive place in the folklore of the Western world. It is the garret under the stars where starving geniuses eke out a shiveringly cold existence, putting their art before comfort and prosperity. It is Peter Pan's land where children can play make-believe games as they discover lost relics of yesteryear, stored away among the family heirlooms in cobweb-covered trunks. Or – who knows? – it is a treasure house where adults might stumble across lost or unknown masterpieces, hidden away under the dust.

Well, coming down to earth – if you can use such a phrase when talking about lofts – it is unlikely in the extreme that the attic in your suburban home can fill any of these fantasies. But, nevertheless, hidden out of sight above your head is a commodity that in these days is very precious indeed. I am talking about living space.

In many houses it is possible for that loft area, lying useless and idle at present, to be converted into extra accommodation, relieving pressure on the space in the rest of the house, adding greatly to the comfort, convenience and facilities of your home, and allowing you and your family to live a fuller, better life.

There are, in fact, three basic ways in which a home can be extended:

You can move outwards, but there are planning difficulties about taking the front of your house beyond the present building line; most of us simply do not have the room at the side of the house; and an extension at the back would encroach on precious garden space.

You can move downwards, but you need to have at least a

rudimentary cellar there to begin with, or be involved in impossibly complex interference with the foundations; then there is the
problem of damp, headroom and letting enough daylight in.

Or you can move upwards, and build a room in the loft. This
type of conversion has so much to commend it. The planning
problems are easier, you are not wasting precious garden space,
you make use of the existing structure of your house, and, because
heat travels upwards rather than sideways, or downwards, an
extension in the loft is the easiest of all to keep warm.

Furthermore, the cost of a loft extension can be substantially
reduced, because large parts of the work can be done on a
do-it-yourself basis. Not all of it, of course. The heavy constructional stuff must be left to a builder. But once the basics have
been completed, then a do-it-yourselfer, even one of fairly limited
abilities, can take over the work and carry it out to a very
satisfactory standard.

Is your loft suitable?

One thing you cannot do yourself is plan your loft extension. This
must be left to an expert. Many local architects, surveyors and
builders are willing to take on this work – in fact, some specialize
in it. And there are national firms, which advertise in the home
magazines, that will carry out loft conversions throughout the
country.

The surveyors offer a leaflet giving information on how they can
help people wishing to extend their home. It is available from the
Information Centre, the Royal Institution of Chartered Surveyors,
12 Great George Street, Parliament Square, London, SW1P
3AD. The Royal Institute of British Architects is at 66 Portland
Place, London, W1N 4AD.

But, long before you reach the stage of talking to an expert
adviser, you ought to devote a lot of thought to your loft
conversion, then do some preliminary planning yourself. The first
thing you must determine is whether the loft in your home is
suitable for conversion. For right at the start I have to strike a sour
note. Unfortunately, many homes are simply not suited to a room
in the loft, and these tend to be modern ones, just the sort where
space is at a premium. For instance, some modern homes have flat
roofs, and with these an extension in the attic is clearly out of the

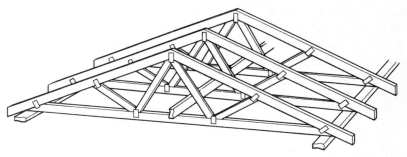

Figure 1   A modern trussed rafter roof (unsuitable for loft conversion)

question. There is no loft, therefore there can be no loft conversion. But, equally, a lot of modern homes with roofs that are sloping – or pitched, to use the proper term – are quite unsuited to loft conversions. These are houses that have roofs known in the jargon of the building trade as being of trussed rafter construction. This type of roof is shown in sketch form in Figure 1. Now in just about every attic you are likely to come across, there will be timber (sometimes even steel) members that form part of the roof construction right in the middle. These will have to be moved – and compensating supports inserted elsewhere – before you can use the space as a living area. But the point about trussed rafters is

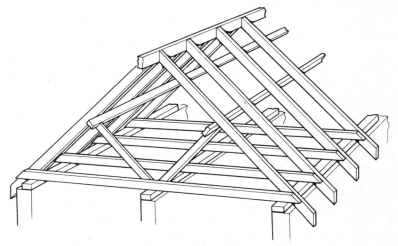

Figure 2   Older style roof (suitable for loft conversion)

that you simply cannot remove the middle trusses ... at least not without bringing the roof down, or carrying out a lot of complicated construction, since each part is so dependent on the other. As a result, there simply will not be a clear area where you can create new rooms in the loft. So if you have a modern house, you would do well to open the trap door into the loft, pop your head up there, shine a torch, and look at the way your roof is built. If you see trussed rafters, then you had better start ringing round the estate agents, and tell them you are looking for a bigger home. Or find some other way of extending your present one.

But if the roof is the kind shown in Figure 2 then a conversion is possible ... with one proviso: there must be enough headroom. So measure the ridge height – i.e. the distance between the top of the ceiling joists and the underside of the ridge board, which runs right at the apex of the roof – X in Figure 3 – to see if it will be possible

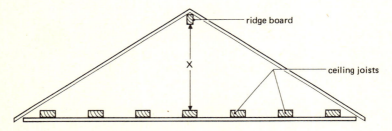

Figure 3   Measuring the ridge height

to create rooms with a minimum ceiling height of 2.3 metres (7 ft 7 in) as required by the Building Regulations. If the answer is yes, you can take your planning a stage further and you could now begin your talks with a surveyor, architect or builder, to discuss the possibilities.

Replanning your home

What are the possibilities? It may well be that all you have in mind is a little extra rudimentary storage. Somewhere to keep out-of-season sports gear, perhaps; the garden furniture in winter; little-used tools and equipment; old clothes and documents you do not want to throw away; the suitcases of a family that travels only once a year for the summer holidays – a sort of 'garden shed in the sky' if you like.

The loft is eminently suitable for this sort of storage and a very simple conversion would suffice. In fact, many of the points I detail in the rest of this chapter would probably not concern you. You might, for instance, not be worried about headroom, letting the daylight in, ventilation – all things to be taken into account when you want to live in your attic.

In fact, you might even arrange some storage in a trussed-rafter attic.

It might be as well to put a floor over at least part of the loft so that you do not have to balance on the joists, with the consequent risk of slipping and damaging the ceiling below, when you are up there. An electric light, perhaps even a power point, would be sensible additions, too. You might, also, have to enlarge the size of the loft opening so that you can take bulkier items through it. You should certainly install a loft ladder so that you can get into and out of your loft with ease and safety. And, as a further safety measure, you should beware of putting inflammable materials in such an out-of-the-way part of your home, although, in fact, research shows that very few domestic fires originate in materials stored in lofts.

One loft that I know has been used as a site for quite an ambitious and extensive model railway layout, and a rudimentary conversion is all that is required for that, too.

It is more than likely, however, that as a reader of this book your plans are much more ambitious than all of these. The reason that you wish to extend your home is more likely to be that you want to increase your actual living space, and, therefore, it will be your intention to create in the loft what are known in the jargon of the business as 'habitable rooms'. What then are the possibilities?

You ought to take this opportunity to rethink the whole scope and purpose of your home. For instance, the most obvious use for rooms in the loft would be as sleeping quarters, and that is fine if the extra bedrooms are to be allocated to, say, teenage children. More than likely the children would spend a lot of their evenings in their bedrooms, and that would mean that your musical tastes would not clash as you listened to the TV or radio on the ground floor, and they played pop records on the top. Then, hopefully, they would have settled down and stopped creating a din by the time you came to retire for the night in the room immediately below theirs.

But if the reason for the extension is that you want to have an elderly relative, on whom you need to keep an eye, come to live with you, then it is not a good idea to have their bedroom in the loft. Climbing two flights of stairs can be quite a strain for an elderly person, and you ought to rearrange the planning of your home so that your granny annexe is on the ground floor. This means that granny will live, perhaps, in what is now your sitting room. In that case your existing bedroom can, perhaps be turned into the living room, and you would then sleep in a new room in the loft. Don't, incidentally, think of resiting the dining room upstairs, at least not unless you intend to take the kitchen with it, as the dining table should always be close to the kitchen. Otherwise you will find yourself having to do a lot of walking up and down the stairs every time you come to serve a meal.

Nor is it a good idea to have a games room on the top floor, especially if the games to be played involve such activities as table tennis and dancing, which would mean a lot of pounding about. For then the sounds would reverberate throughout the home, and eventually almost certainly damage the ceiling below. Ping pong and jiving are best confined to the ground floor – and, preferably, a solid one at that.

The loft would seem to be an ideal situation for a hobbies room. It is out of the way, and you do not have to tidy up every time you break off work for the day. But, once again, it depends what the hobbies are. If they are largely sedentary, such as study, philately, delicate crafts, or whatever, then fine. But if they involve the use of large materials such as long lengths of timber, heavy ones such as might be required in some forms of sculpture, or dirty ones as in pottery ... well, it simply is not a good idea to have to drag these right through the rest of the home and up two flights of stairs.

If you live in an area of outstanding beauty, or even just overlooking the local cricket field or tennis courts, then one of the best uses for your loft would be as a sitting room so you could take advantage of the view.

It is not advisable, however, to include in your plans a room that requires a water supply, because, for reasons I explain in Chapter 4, the water pressure in the loft would be very low, and water would merely trickle out of the taps instead of flowing freely. You would certainly never get a satisfactory shower there, for instance. A booster pump would overcome some of the problems, but it is better to avoid the necessity for it if you can by siting kitchens and bathrooms lower down in the house.

The regulations

If you are going to use your loft just for random storage, then you can go right ahead with your plans. You do not need permission from anybody, and you hardly need worry about any form of conversion, except the few simple additions I have already detailed. However, should you intend to convert it to habitable purposes, then you must get approval from the appropriate authorities, and you must comply fully with all the rules and regulations.

What are these rules? They are very complex, and it is doubtful whether you could find your way through the minefield of them without expert help. For instance, with your loft conversion you are turning a two-storey building into a three-storey one (unless, of course, you start off with a bungalow). That, for a start, brings you into a whole new area of fire regulations. One thing that will probably mean is that you will have to fit automatic closers to all your doors. Types suitable for do-it-yourself fixing are available at ironmongers and come with full instructions.

But don't worry. It will be the job of your architect, or other adviser, to see that your work does not break the law. He will draw up plans, submit them to the relevant authority, and get them passed.

However, it is a good idea for you to have some notion of the problems involved, to help you in your initial planning, and also so that you can expound your ideas more fully when you come to brief your expert adviser.

There are, in fact, two sets of rules that govern building in Britain – the planning laws and the Building Regulations. The difference between the two is a little complex but, broadly speaking, the former stipulate what you can build where, whilst the latter state how the work must be carried out, in the form of the construction methods and materials that may be used. And if that is a little of an oversimplification, it is good enough for our present purposes. In Inner London, the London Building

Acts take the place of the Building Regulations. They are similar, but in many instances more strict, and special procedures apply. Your architect will know all about them. Scotland, too, has its own rules.

I mention the planning regulations, but you should, in fact, have no trouble over planning permission with your loft extension because this is, in the planner's jargon, a permitted development. The Planning Acts allow you to increase the volume of your house by up to 70 cu m (2472 cu ft) or 15 per cent of the original size of the house to a maximum of 115 cu m (4060 cu ft) whichever is the greater, without planning permission. But the point about building a room in the loft is that you are not increasing the size of your house just making use of the space that would otherwise be wasted. Dormers, of course, make the house bigger, but you could add a lot of these without breaking through the restrictions.

The only difficulty would come if your home already has an extension of some sort, for this, unless it were built before 1948, would not count as the original house, and permission for it might have been granted on condition that no further development took place.

Permission will be needed if your conversion would raise the height of the building, but there will be no problem on that score if you keep it below the existing height of the roof ridge. Or if it were to extend beyond the front building line – again something you can avoid. In a conservation area, or if your home is a listed building, there could be problems but by and large no planning trouble need be anticipated, although you might like to have a word with the appropriate officials at your local town hall, even before talking to an architect.

With the Building Regulations, however, it is a different story. They will govern every part of your conversion, laying down which materials you can use, and the methods of construction you have to adopt. You must get Building Regulation approval before work begins, and the Building Control Officers will visit the site whilst work is in progress to inspect things. But here, too, your architect will advise you on these matters and ensure that your plans comply with the regulations. From the start your local authority will want to be convinced that your house structure, and in particular the roof, is strong enough to stand up to any strain that will be

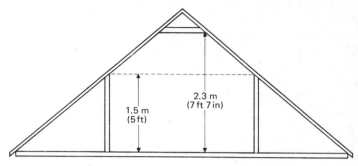

Figure 4   Measuring ceiling height

imposed by the conversion, and many of them have been very sticky on this point in recent years.

Once again it might be as well if we take a look at some of the regulations to help you in your initial thoughts, and the discussions you will need to have with your architect.

The most important is the rule that your new room must have a minimum ceiling height of 2.3 m (7 ft 7 in) over at least half its area, as measured on an imaginary plane 1.5 m (5 ft) above the floor (Figure 4).

When you first poke your head through the trap door into the loft and peer through the gloom and dust, these rules may seem to make any room in your loft impossibly small. But don't worry. You can install dormer windows, as Figure 5 shows, and you

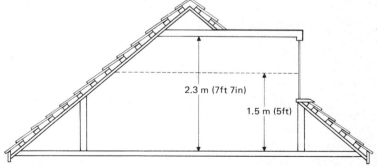

Figure 5   A dormer window may increase the space available for conversion

immediately increase the scope of your conversion. To get enough space you may have to fit one at the front and back of the house. Incidentally, your only experience of dormers may be the tiny ones you get in quaint cottages and old inns, where the overall impression is of nooks and crannies and steeply sloping ceilings. The atmosphere inside a modern room with dormers is totally different. In fact, if a dormer spans one whole wall you would never guess from the inside that the roof is at the side, and not on top, of the room.

Dormer windows at the same time solve another problem – that of letting daylight into your loft. However, the installation of dormers is not a job for the amateur – it is precisely the sort of heavy constructional work that must be left to a builder.

Figure 6   Roof window

Where headroom is really limited you can consider fitting a hollow-joisted ceiling instead of the conventional kind. This type of ceiling is simply one in which the plaster is fixed to the top of the joists instead of the underside. The point about it is that the height of the room is measured to the plaster, not the underside of the joists. Thus you are gaining the thickness of the joists and of the plaster. Such a ceiling can look quite attractive if the joists are stained a dark colour, and the plaster in between them painted white. In fact, it could give a period flavour to your conversion.

There is another type of window suitable for loft conversion, and this is the roof window (Figure 6). It does not give you any extra headroom, but is much cheaper than a dormer, and even fairly unskilled do-it-yourselfers can fit this type of window themselves. If you can get a big enough room without the use of dormers, you should consider fitting a roof window, for this will considerably reduce the cost of the work.

The Building Regulations also have a thing or two to say about ventilation in your conversion. The opening parts of the window(s), together with any air bricks in the new room, must have a combined area equal to at least one twentieth of the total room area – again calculated on that imaginary plane 1.5 m (5 ft) above the floor. Furthermore, some part of this ventilation must be more than 1.75 m (5 ft 9 in) above the floor. And you must make sure that it is well clear of chimneys, flues, and the soil pipes of the lavatory, so that obnoxious fumes and gases are not sucked into the room.

Any chimneys that do get in the way could be dispensed with, if you no longer use them, by being capped at the top, and blocked

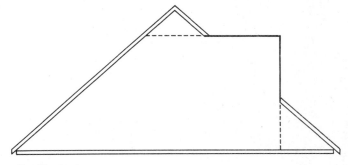

Figure 7   Single dormer

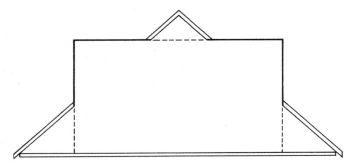

Figure 8   Through dormer

off down in the house with perhaps the fireplace and hearth removed to make more space. Soil pipes, too, can be repositioned. But all of this would add to the cost of your conversion.

Dormer windows

But back to dormers. There are, in fact, three basic types – the single dormer (Figure 7); the through dormer (Figure 8) and the bay dormer (Figure 9), which reaches to the outside wall of the house. The latter can incorporate picture windows in the right sort of situation – a site that is not overlooked, or has a view. But if you are surrounded by other homes, and a fully glazed dormer would mean a loss of privacy, you could have an infill panel below waist-high windows.

A balcony outside the windows (Figure 10) is a possibility with the first two types, and would be a handsome addition to the

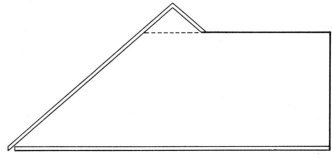

Figure 9   Bay dormer

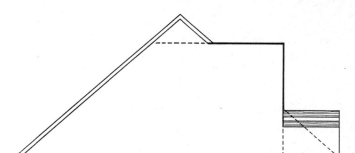

Figure 10   Single dormer with balcony

amenities of your home in the right sort of situation.

How big an area your loft conversion will cover depends on the shape of the roof as well as the floor area of the loft. For instance, take the three houses shown in Figure 11, all of which we will assume to have the same floor area. The dotted lines show the space available for conversion. The detached house has a hip (that's the building trade's jargon for the sloping bit) at each end. Only the space between the hips can be used unless dormers are also inserted in the hips. The semi-detached house has only one hip, so more space is freed for the room in the loft. There are no

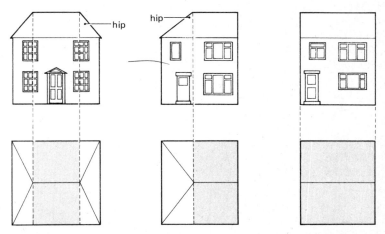

Figure 11   Only the space within the dotted lines is available for conversion

hips at all on the roof of the terraced house, therefore the whole loft area is available for conversion. Many detached and semi-detached houses, of course, have straight gable ends, without a hip.

Means of access

One of the most important aspects of your loft conversion will be the means of access to it. You can create the most beautiful rooms imaginable up there but, if you do not have a staircase so that you can reach them, the whole thing would be laughably pointless.

If you are using the loft just for junk storage, you can fit merely a loft ladder – the sort that is attached to the back of the trap door, and slides or folds down when, with the aid of a pole-hook, you open the door. Loft ladders, however, are quite out of the question when the loft will contain habitable rooms – as are other makeshifts such as rope ladders. The Building Regulations will simply not allow them; you must have a proper staircase. The regulations also lay down stringent rules about staircases – their size, slope, and the headroom you must leave above them, for instance. Your architect will know all about these rules, and make sure that your conversion conforms to them.

Fitting a staircase into the existing top floor of your home is no easy matter, as you will discover when you get down to some preliminary planning, and you may have to sacrifice rather more space here than you had bargained for. In fact, in some instances, dormer windows are installed not so much to give extra headroom and more daylight in your loft, but to allow a staircase to be fitted in without too much upheaval to the lower storeys of the house.

In many homes the best position for a new staircase is directly over the existing one, and you can if you wish make your new stairway an open tread one, so that, visually, it will dominate the landing much less.

Many people imagine they can overcome all the problems of finding room for a staircase by fitting a spiral one, for there is a common misconception that these take up less room. In fact they don't. It is merely that the space they occupy is of a different shape – squarish as opposed to the rectangle of a conventional staircase. This fact, of course, means that they can solve the problem of fitting a staircase into some homes – where, for instance, there is a definite square area going spare on the first-floor landing. And it is undeniable that they have a certain eye-catching visual appeal. However, there are drawbacks. For a start, the fact that the treads are very narrow near the centre of the staircase makes them awkward to use, especially for the very young, and the infirm. Moreover, it is not easy to take furniture up them – can you imagine trying to struggle up one with a double bed? They are also much more tricky to manufacture than ordinary stairs, and consequently are dearer. They are, too, more difficult to fit – one could not recommend their installation by a do-it-yourselfer.

So, all in all, in most homes you will probably find it best to fit a conventional staircase, and the best place for this will probably be over the existing one. That may well mean encroaching somewhat on one of the present first-floor bedrooms, but it cannot be helped. You will have to discuss the matter fully with your adviser.

Heating systems

Your new room(s) will, of course, need to be heated. If you have central heating at present, then the best way is to add one or more radiators to your existing system, always assuming that there is enough spare capacity in the boiler to power them. Contact the man who installed your present system, and tell him what you propose to do. He will then say if your present boiler is big enough, and will also plot a way to connect up the new radiators to the existing pipework. If you do not know who installed your heating, or cannot get in touch with him, then consult another heating engineer. Your architect or other adviser can help here.

Hopefully, there will be enough spare capacity, since the people who design and install central heating systems usually leave a little leeway. But if your boiler is hard put to it to keep the present system working satisfactorily, then the addition of extra radiators will mean you will have to reconcile yourself to lower temperatures throughout, or you will have to install a bigger boiler.

Another possibility is to use gas fires – always assuming that gas is laid on in the house. They, of course, have to be fitted by an expert – a do-it-yourselfer should never tamper with gas. Or you could use electric fires. However electricity is a very expensive fuel to use for space heating. Fitting the socket outlets for these is definitely a job you can tackle, as we shall see in Chapter 7.

You will probably want to avoid solid fuel fires. Apart from the extra cost and trouble of having a chimney and fireplace installed, you will find it's no fun carrying a loaded coal bucket up three storeys, and bringing the ashes down again.

One very important point: whatever type of heating you choose, do make sure your extension is well insulated. In fact, your local authority will insist on it. Ways of insulating the conversion are discussed in Chapter 6. So ... there you are. Having read all the foregoing information you should be able to work out a clear idea of what you would like to do with your home. You will then be in a position to talk to an architect, surveyor or other specialist. Right at the start, tell him that you want to do as much of the work yourself as possible, leaving only the main structural tasks to a builder. Don't be afraid of doing this. You will find most architects and surveyors only too willing to cooperate with do-it-yourself projects.

Your adviser will help you to choose a builder. He may well put out the work to tender, or ask two or more firms to submit estimates. Then he will advise you on which is the most suitable.

Leave it to the builder

Let us sum up what the builder must do. It will be necessary for him to clear out the centre of your existing loft, getting rid of support members for the roof that are in the way, so that there will be enough room for your loft conversion. He will in all probability have to add extra support to other parts of the rafters. It is essential that this work is left to a builder, guided by your architect or surveyor. It is utterly out of the question for the average do-it-yourselfer to undertake work of this kind.

You must leave to him, too, the job of carrying out any strengthening work needed for the joists. After all, whoever built your house calculated that these would have to bear only the weight of the ceiling below. If they have, in addition, to support a floor, and all the things that will stand on it, reinforcement may be needed.

And should you be having dormer windows, then these too must be fitted by your builder.

However, with this main work out of the way, there is no reason whatever why you should not go on and carry out the remainder of the conversion yourself. In the other chapters of this book, I will detail exactly what has to be done if you wish to do certain jobs yourself. It is up to you to read the instructions carefully, and decide if you are capable of undertaking them.

If you feel any of them are beyond you, then tell your architect, and ask him to add them to the builder's schedule. The rest, you can get on with yourself.

For further information on loft conversion in general (not the d-i-y aspect) contact the National Home Enlargement Bureau, PO Box 67, High Wycombe, Bucks. HP15 6XP.

How to pay for it all

It is all very well to talk about the work that has to be done, and to discuss how much of it you can do yourself, but for many people there will be an even more troublesome question: how do I pay for it all? And the answer is that you find the money to enlarge your present house in just the same way you would raise it if you were getting a bigger house by moving – i.e. you borrow it.

Raising a loan for home improvement works is eminently possible, and building a loft extension is an improvement that qualifies for such loans. Remember, too, that the interest you pay on money borrowed for improving your home – as opposed to merely carrying out maintenance work – qualifies for tax relief just as surely as the money you borrowed to buy your home in the first place. This means that, broadly speaking, under present regulations you can claim relief on interest paid on loans that total altogether up to £25,000. Your local tax office – or an accountant – will advise you. Anyway here are some possibilities:

Building societies: Whenever it is at all possible you should always try to borrow money for home improvements work from a building society. For not only will the society charge just about the lowest rate of interest you can find, but also you will probably be given the longest repayment period, so that your monthly payments will be the lowest of all, and thus much more manageable. Of course, it isn't always possible. Building societies regard loaning money for house purchase, rather than improvement, as being their main purpose, and when funds are light they are likely to give priority to home buyers, especially first-time ones, or others with an urgent reason for moving. Nevertheless, in your search for a loan for your loft extension, the first person you should approach is your building society manager. There are occasions when building societies are so flush with money that they welcome this type of business, and, even when times are hard, if you have a 'compassionate' reason for extending your loft – such as a growing family desperate for more living space, or an elderly relative who has to come and live with you – you will still get a sympathetic hearing.

One problem is that some building society branch managers do not like to lend money for work that will be done on a do-it-yourself basis. They fear that the workmanship will be of such a poor quality that it will lower the value of your home. And since the house is the security for the money they have lent you, this is of vital importance to them. Those of us in the home improvement business know that their fears are usually groundless; that someone working on his own home, in which he and his wife will live, and his children grow up, is much more likely to take the care and trouble needed to produce a top-class result, than a professional who, no matter how conscientious, is only doing a job, and cannot have the same interest in the work. But ... there you are.

Your loan from a building society can take the form of either an extension to your existing mortgage, should you have one and should it have some time to run, or it can be an entirely new mortgage.

In any event, the society will want to carry out a survey just as it does when granting a mortgage to finance an original purchase, in order to determine how valuable your house will be after the conversion. And it will expect you to pay for this, and for the legal fees incurred in drawing up the mortgage. Do not, incidentally, confuse these fees with those involved in the conveyancing of your house when you first bought it. The legal fees associated with just the mortgage are minimal. It will also make enquiries about your earnings to be sure you can afford the repayments, and your total borrowing – i.e. the new loan and whatever you still owe on the mortgage – must not exceed any maximum that the society is applying at the moment.

Banks: If you cannot get a loan from a building society, your next move should be to see your bank manager, for the banks are anxious to compete with the building societies in lending money for both home buying and improvements. In fact, some of them are specifically advertising home improvement loans. Terms and conditions vary, but a typical scheme would grant a loan of £3,000 over any period from six months to three years, perhaps even longer. Such a loan will probably be a 'personal' one in that the bank would be more interested in your financial standing and your ability to repay, rather than what you wanted the money for, although the manager would certainly want to hear about your plans. The trouble is that £3,000 does not buy all that much home improvement nowadays, and if you need more than that you would be into an area where some form of security was asked for. This might well take the form of a second mortgage on your home, unless you have some other security.

Bank interest is, of course, usually higher than that charged by building societies but, where money for mortgages is concerned, the gap between the building society and bank interest seems to be narrowing all the time – in fact, there are cases where some banks claim their rate is lower – and when you take into account the tax relief perhaps the difference is not so vital, after all.

Finance companies: You can get a home improvement loan from a finance company. They, like the banks, have schemes aimed specifically at the home improver. Repayment periods are often the same as at banks, but the interest is higher.

Credit cards: One would not normally go seeking a home improvement loan from a credit card company – apart from anything else, the maximum advance is usually far too low. There are cases, however, where it would be appropriate to do so. For example, your building society might grant a mortgage only for the heavy constructional work being carried out by a builder. In that case, remember that builders' merchants and electrical and plumbing suppliers often accept credit cards, and you could pay by this method for the materials to carry out the finishing touches. Secondly, you might be carrying out only a rudimentary conversion – a loft ladder, small area of flooring, with perhaps an electric light and a power point. You could easily pay for the raw materials for such work with a credit card.

Improvement grants

Can you get a Home Improvement Grant to help you pay for your loft conversion? It is not very likely. A few grants have been paid by some local authorities for this type of work in the past, but others tell me that they have never made a grant towards a room in the loft. And, increasingly in the future, you will be met by a refusal if you apply for one. Local authorities are under great pressure to reduce their spending, and any money they have available for Home Improvement Grants will go more and more towards helping owners of run-down homes provide the basics – hot water, bathroom, proper heating and so on. The only occasion on which you might get a sympathetic hearing would be if you had a very small house along with a large family, and an extra room or two would be the only way in which you might house your dependants adequately. Otherwise, I'm afraid it is going to be the thumbs down sign.

Another type of grant available to householders is that to help them pay for the cost of laying down loft insulation, in a home where there is no such insulation at present. The scheme provides grants of two thirds, up to a maximum of £50, of the cost of loft insulation, lagging cold water pipes and tanks in the roof, and insulating the hot water cylinder. For elderly people on low incomes, a grant of up to 90 per cent with a maximum of £90 can be paid. Well, your loft extension will need to be insulated, as we shall see later on when we get down to the construction work. Will you qualify for a grant? The answer is . . . it depends. For the rules are quite specific. If there is any insulation in your loft at present, you cannot have a grant. If there is none, you might qualify. And those rules apply to homes whether they have a loft extension or not. So if you had insulation down in your loft before you started to convert it, there is no point in your applying. If you had no insulation, go along and see your local council.

But in any event the cuts in local authority spending mean that there is less and less money available for this type of work.

For full information on grants, enquire at your local town hall.

2
The Windows

Your loft conversion will need windows just as surely as the rest of the living rooms in your home, not only to let in the light, but also to provide adequate ventilation, in order to comply with the Building Regulations, as explained in Chapter 1. In certain areas, other means of ventilation, such as extractor fans and grilles, are suitable, but in living rooms and, perhaps more especially, bedrooms, nothing beats the appeal of an open window.

Two types of window are suitable for a loft – dormer windows, and roof windows. Installing them is one of the first jobs to be tackled, for two reasons. Firstly – and this is especially true of dormers – installation of the windows will usually be a job you will leave to your builder, who will undertake it as part of his initial preparation work. Secondly, once the windows are in there will be more daylight in your loft, and you will be able to see more clearly what you are doing.

Since dormers are the most popular type of loft window, let us look at them first.

Dormer windows

Installing a dormer is definitely a job you should leave to your builder, unless you happen to be a very skilled and experienced do-it-yourselfer. For the work involves interfering with the structural members of the roof and, unless you know what you are doing, you could cause serious damage. Furthermore, it can be a bit tricky ensuring a waterproof seal all the way round the dormer. In fact, installing the dormer is probably a job that the builder will see as part of the heavy constructional work of modifying the roof structure to leave the way clear for your finishing touches. Try to persuade your architect to take some care and trouble over the design of your dormers, for they can affect the whole look of your home. If they are properly integrated into the architectural style of the building then they will add to its appearance and value, making it more attractive than it is at present. But if they look as though they have been stuck on as an afterthought, they can be an eyesore. It is not an easy job to design a good-looking dormer, for after all its main purpose is to give you the correct amount of headroom inside the loft, and that can conflict with many other design considerations. However, it does help when the exterior of the dormer – both its roof and sides – are clad in materials that tone in with the rest of the roof. This might in some cases put up the cost, but that is surely worth it to give you a more attractive – and valuable – home.

For the actual window itself, your architect and/or builder will probably use a standard item because this will make the job cheaper and, indeed, the dormer will in all probability be built round a standard size window frame. This frame, too, should match the appearance of those in the rest of the house. For instance, aluminium sliding window frames can look very attractive, and there is also the bonus that they need little in the way of maintenance. But if elsewhere you have traditional-style timber frames, then an aluminium frame in your dormer will look like an alien intrusion. However, if you have metal frames – either steel or aluminium – lower down the house, these are what ought to be specified for your extension. Matching up may, however, not be so easy if you want to fit a balcony in front of your dormer, for the windows that lead on to it ought to be sliding, since these will take up less balcony space than the traditional french doors, which open outwards. Timber-framed patio doors are available, but it might be more convenient to have the aluminium kind.

As for the actual panes themselves, since the windows are being installed from scratch, it will cost you very little extra to have double glazing, something that is very worthwhile for a loft which will be one of the most exposed parts of your home. In a new installation you can fit a sealed double glazed unit – i.e. one that consists of two panes of glass that are fused together at the factory, to form one, with a hermetically sealed air space in between. Such sealed units cannot in general be fitted to existing frames, but there is no problem when you are building a window from scratch. It would make your loft a warmer place and, in the case of a very large window, cut down on fuel bills.

The fitting of the actual window frame, once the dormer has been built, is a job that many, if not most, do-it-yourselfers could tackle. However, I doubt if your builder would lower his charges sufficiently, if you offered to fit the frames yourself, to make it worth your while. However, fixing the plasterboard to the inner walls and ceiling of the dormer is something that you should ask him to leave for you to do, since this will form part of building the shell of the room (Chapter 6).

Installing roof windows

The other window suitable for loft conversions is the type that can actually be fitted into the slope of a roof, and is known as a roof window. It is well worth considering if you can get enough headroom without a dormer. One of its main advantages is that you can fit it without the extra building work and the amount of disturbance to the roof structure that a dormer calls for, and its installation is therefore less costly, even when carried out by a builder. But, more than that, modern roof windows have been expressly designed for easy installation, and provided you are dealing with one of the smaller models, or have a friend to help you if your plans call for a larger one, they can be fitted by a skilled do-it-yourselfer. Full instructions are supplied by the manufacturers, but let me give you an idea of what is involved, then you can see if you feel able to tackle it.

You have, of course, to cut an opening for the window in your roof. Obviously, you need to get such a hole covered as quickly as possible, otherwise you risk having rain come through. So do as much of the initial work as possible beforehand. Have the window ready in the loft, assemble the correct tools, and prepare the extra timber supports etc. Then it should be possible to install the window in a day.

It is easy to get a watertight fit with a modern roof light because of the flashing that is supplied. The window is fixed by means of brackets to the rafters (Figure 12), so from the wide range of sizes available choose one that will fit the spacing of the rafters in your

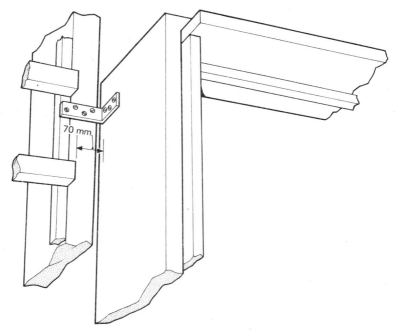

Figure 12   A roof window is fixed to the rafters by brackets

roof. If your architect specifies a window wider than this spacing you will have to cut a gap in one or more of the rafters. In that case, the cut rafter will need to be properly supported, and trimmers inserted (Figure 13). This is not a particularly difficult job, but it must be done properly otherwise you risk weakening the whole roof, so do not embark on it unless you feel confident that you know what you are doing.

Before you can understand exactly how to make the opening a quick description of how roofs are constructed is necessary (Figure 14). The roof covering will consist of slates or tiles, both of which are fixed to a series of battens nailed across the rafters. The distance between the battens is governed by the size of the slates or tiles, and the amount by which they overlap, which in turn will be determined by the roof's slope (or pitch to give it the correct term). Slates are nailed to a batten at either their centre or their top, and there should be two nails to each slate. The nails are normally of copper, aluminium or a mixture of zinc and copper.

Tiles have a couple of projecting nibs at their top, and these hook over the battens. Each tile also has two nail holes, but normally only every third or fourth course of tile is nailed, those in between being held in place by the nibs and the weight of the overlapping tiles.

In well-built houses a lining of felt is laid under the tiles and battens and is held in place by the battens, the fixing nails of which are driven through the felt. The felt is laid lengthways across the rafters, and fixed loosely so that it sags slightly between them, to form a channel down which any water that gets through the slates or tiles can run safely away. So that water cannot get under the felt, the top roll overlaps the next one lower down, and so on.

In some of the better-class properties of the thirties – just the sort suitable for a loft conversion – tongued and grooved boards were fixed under the felt to provide a really strong, weatherproof roof, although the practice was never all that common. A quick

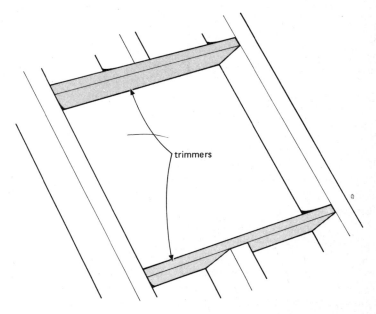

Figure 13   If a rafter has to be cut, it must be properly supported by trimmers

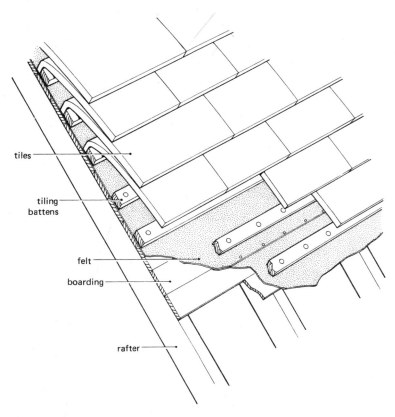

tiles

tiling
battens

felt

boarding

rafter

Figure 14   How a roof is constructed

glance at the underside of your roof when you make your first
inspection will tell you how yours is built. You will see either
boards, felt, or the underside of the slates or tiles themselves.

Begin the installation by marking on the underside of the roof
the outline of the hole you need to cut. You must make sure that
you position the window so that you have a row of whole tiles or
slates at the bottom. Both tiles and slates can be cut at the top and
sides of the opening, to give an opening of the correct size, but
never at the bottom. Then start to cut out the hole. Boards should
be tackled with a portable circular saw, its blade depth set so that it
just cuts through the thickness of the board, and does not protrude

too much on the other side. The felt is best cut with a sharp knife. Determine the centre of the hole, and from this point make four knife cuts in the felt, one to each of the four corners. This creates four triangles which are later folded back against the sides of your new window frame, and trimmed.

Next you can start on the slates or tiles. To take these off you have to get rid of the nails holding them in place, and you do this with a slater's ripping tool. This has a handle and a long blade that widens out at the end. Push the blade under the tiles, slip its end round a nail, give a sharp tug, and the nail will come loose, allowing you to free the slate or tile. Getting rid of your first few slates will be a bit tricky and there is the danger that one or two of them might slip, and crash to the ground, so you must take every precaution to ensure that no one is standing in the danger zone. Once you can poke your head through the hole you will get on a

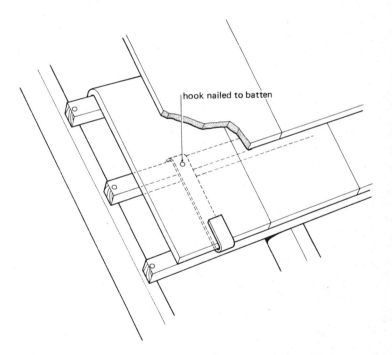

hook nailed to batten

Figure 15   When fitting tiles back in place, it may be necessary to make up a hook as shown here

lot better. Don't discard any of these slates yet for you will need some to make good around the opening once the window is in place. As you work you might have to adjust slightly the position of the hole, to ensure that you get a row of whole tiles at the bottom.

Once all the slates have been removed, you can saw out any section of rafters that need to be removed. Before you do so, you must provide temporary support to those that will be cut, by running a stout prop between the rafter and a ceiling joist below. Preferably, the prop should be screwed to both joist and rafter. Next fix the trimmers, and you can remove the supports.

Install the window and its flashing in accordance with the manufacturer's instructions. Note that the glazed sash is removed from the frame, and placed carefully on one side while you install the frame. This makes the assembly lighter and easier to handle.

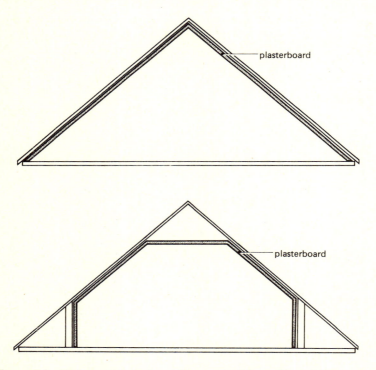

Figure 16   With a roof window, all or part of the ceiling of the new room(s) may be fixed to existing rafters

Finally put back any slates or tiles as needed to neaten off the opening.

These slates might be difficult to fix, depending on where the overlaps come, and how accessible the nail holes are. You might find it easier to make a fixing by drilling new nail holes. Otherwise, make up a hook as shown (Figure 15) from aluminium, copper or lead. One end hooks over a convenient batten, the other holds the slate in place.

With a roof window instead of a dormer, you may well find you will fix at least part of the ceiling of your new rooms to the existing rafters of the roof instead of having to build a framework of new joists. Some possibilities are shown in Figure 16.

This will result in another saving on the cost of your conversion. It is still vital, however, to put sufficient insulation behind the plasterboard.

For more information on roof lights contact The Velux Co. Ltd, Telford Road, Eastfield Industrial Estate, Glenrothes, Fife KY7 4NX.

3

Getting Up There

Your loft extension will, quite patently, be of no use unless you can actually get into it, so the design will call for a means of access. Where the loft is to be used just for the storage of junk, then all manner of expedients will do. You can buy a proprietary loft ladder, which is fitted to the trap door into the loft (the door has to be hinged) and operated by a pole with a hook on the end. Some people even get by with a rope ladder, although I feel that this is dangerous unless used by only the young and extremely agile. Some make use of the household steps and use a great deal of energy to haul themselves up, then miraculously survive as they precariously lower themselves down on to the top of the steps when leaving the loft. I have seen cut-down versions of an ordinary builder's timber ladder fixed permanently in place.

If you propose to adopt any of these expedients, do make sure they are properly fixed. The weight of someone climbing up a ladder will put a great strain on its fixings. A couple or so of short, thin screws are not enough to hold a rope ladder or builder's ladder in place. If the ladders are to be fixed to a wall, make sure it is a sound one of solid masonry, in which you can get a firm fixing, and use wall bolts instead of plugs. Should the fixing be to timber, then if possible aim to use thick nuts and bolts. A builder's ladder should be fixed at the bottom as well as the top. Stout brackets bolted to its sides, then fixed to the floor, would be a good idea. Remember you can get a very nasty injury if you fall down from a ladder – you could even cripple yourself. It simply is not worth taking a gamble with your future in this way just for the sake of avoiding the small extra amount of trouble, and the minimal extra expense, a proper fixing would take. So always err on the side of safety. As for loft ladders, I will take a fuller look at these later on in this chapter.

Fitting a staircase

When your extension incorporates fully habitable rooms, it must have a proper staircase, such as you already have to get from the ground floor to the first. Finding room to fit in such a staircase is one of the trickiest parts of the whole design, for there is no doubt that a staircase takes up a lot of space, and if you are not careful you will find it using up just as much as you have gained with your extra room in the loft. Your architect will know how to deal with these problems.

Obviously, the stairs cannot just lead to nowhere. You need a hole in the existing top-floor ceiling, so that you can emerge from the stairs and into the loft. Making such a hole is a job within the scope of the do-it-yourselfer.

You may well have some form of opening already, for most homes have a door into the loft. It is hardly likely that such an opening will be large enough, however, to allow materials to be carried up into the loft in the first place, let alone to take a staircase. In any event, it will probably not be in the right place so a new one must be cut, and this is how you do it. The following instructions are written on the assumption that you already have some sort of access to your loft. Where this is not so, you will have to adapt them to carry out all the work from below.

First, you – or more likely, your architect – must plot exactly where the opening is to be. Ideally, two opposite sides of the opening should be close to two ceiling joists. Draw its outline on the ceiling, making sure that this is square by using a set square. A good check is to measure the diagonals of the outline. Only if these are equal is the outline truly square. Now drive panel pins up through each corner of the outline, making sure they protrude through the ceiling. Then you will be able to see from inside the loft exactly where each corner of the opening is positioned.

Your ceiling will need support whilst you are working on it. So at one end of the proposed opening place a 50 mm (2 in) thick piece of wood on the floor, hold another similar piece at ceiling level, and wedge a stout post between the two. The timber at ceiling level should run across the ceiling joists. Repeat this arrangement at the other end. Now, working from inside the loft, get rid of any parts of the joist that run across your proposed opening, by sawing through them. Carefully pull the waste away from the ceiling.

The cut ends of the joists cannot just be left dangling loose; they must be supported. The way to do that is to run lengths of timber – known technically as trimmers – between the nearest uncut joists, and across the ends of those you have cut. These trimmers should be of timber the same size as the existing joists – in fact, you might be able to make use of the waste you have cut from the joists. The trimmers are fixed in place with two 100 mm (4 in) round-wire nails at each joint. However, such fixing is firm enough only if all the ends have been sawn truly square, and you might prefer to use instead notched joints over bearers screwed to the sides of the timber.

Where the opening does not exactly coincide with the joists, you can square it off by fitting what is known as a tailer, fixed in just the same way as the trimmers. All these timbers are shown in Figure 17.

With the framework completed the ceiling no longer needs to be

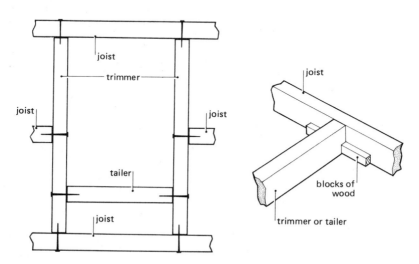

Figure 17   Construction of the opening for the staircase

supported, so you can get rid of the support posts. Clean up all the dust and dirt from on top of your proposed opening, so that it will not cascade through on to the floor below when you cut out the profile. Now begin cutting the opening using a panel saw. If the ceiling is of plasterboard, saw through two opposite sides first. Thread two pieces of string, one at each end, through the saw cuts, and tie them to a nail driven into a joist. This will support the plasterboard, and stop it from crashing down when you cut the opening out completely. If you have lath and plaster, this same dodge might work, but you are more likely to get a cascade of rubbish crashing down on your landing, so be prepared for this. In any event, cut carefully through each lath.

When the opening is fully cut out, the sides of the exposed joists, trimmers and tailers will need to be lined with a timber, which may well incorporate some decorative moulding, according to the design of your architect. Such final detail might, however, best be left until the stairs are fixed. Later you will have to make good with plaster or cellulose filler, before you redecorate.

What are the differences in procedure if you do not already have a trap door into your loft? For a start you might not be able to see exactly where your ceiling joists are, and thus have difficulty in positioning the opening in the correct spot, although on very old ceilings the outline of the joists can often be seen through the lath and plaster. It might be as well in such instances to make a few test borings with a drill to locate the joists, and even cut out a patch of plaster so that you can see where you are working.

You might, in fact, have to cut out the whole of the opening in the plaster before you can cut through the joists, and fit the trimmers. The other problem is that you will be covered with dirt as you work for it will shower down on you when you start to cut through the ceiling, especially if it is of lath and plaster. Should your existing opening be in the correct place, but not big enough, then you enlarge it in pretty much the same way.

When you have finished making the opening, the stairs can be fitted in place. Exactly how this will be done will depend on the layout of your home, and your architect will advise you on this. He will, where possible, make use of a staircase bought ready made from a joinery supplier, rather than involve you in the cost of a purpose-built one.

Can you fit a staircase yourself? It depends – on the complexity of the stairs, and your own skills as a carpenter. I would say that if you have had a fair amount of experience as a do-it-yourselfer, then installing a straight run of stairs would not present you with a problem, but a more complicated staircase might well be beyond

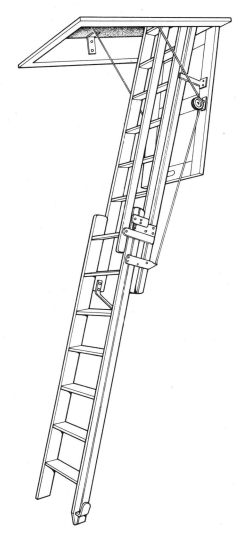

Figure 18a   Sectional loft ladder

your capabilities. The best thing to do is discuss the matter with your architect, and find out what is involved. I am sorry if I seem to be glossing over this problem, but, really, there are so many possibilities and imponderables that it is difficult to be specific. There is one thing you can be sure of, however – your local Building Control Officer will insist on a safe and properly installed staircase. And rightly so, for one that is badly installed is a very dangerous thing indeed.

For information on ready-made staircases contact Magnet and Southern Ltd, Royd Ings Avenue, Keighley, West Yorkshire, BD21 4BY.

Assuming that you have cut a new hole in the ceiling, and not enlarged one you already have, the existing trap door into the loft will now be redundant, and should be dispensed with. The exact construction of such openings does vary, but the following is the basic method of blocking it off. You will have to adapt it to fit your own circumstances.

Take off the door by withdrawing the screws that hold its hinges to the frame. Now get rid of the lining round the opening. This will be merely nailed in place, and you prise it off with an old screwdriver or chisel.

The hole is patched with plasterboard, screwed or nailed in the way described for building the walls of your loft extension (Chapter 6). If the ceiling is of plasterboard, try to use board of the same thickness for the patch, so that it will be level with its surrounding area. Fix the patch to the joists along two opposite sides. The other sides can probably be nailed to supports inserted to take the original lining of the opening. If not fit cross members between the joists. There will be a gap between the old board and the new, which you fill as described for the joint treatment in Chapter 6 (page 73).

A lath and plaster ceiling will probably be a little thicker than the plasterboard patch. You can bring everything to the same level by first nailing thin strips of wood to the joists.

Loft ladders

If you decide on a loft ladder, there are two types from which you can choose – concertina ladders, which work on the 'lazy tongs' principle, and sectional ladders, which operate like ordinary extending ladders, with one section sliding over another. The two types are shown in Figures 18. Both, these days, are usually made from strong, rust-proof aluminium alloy, so very little maintenance is needed. However, it is possible to find sectional ones made from timber. You might want to paint these, or leave them natural.

To operate a loft ladder, you use a pole with a hook on the end

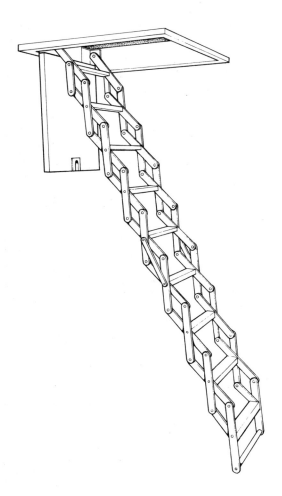

Figure 18b   Concertina loft ladder

of it (supplied by the manufacturer, but – beware – not always included in the basic price). This hook opens the trap door into the loft. The trap must open downwards, so this usually means that you have to modify the operation of an existing door. Then you take hold of the ladder with the pole, and draw it down from its stored position. With the concertina type, you simply pull until the ladder is fully extended. Sectional ladders have safety catches that you release so that the ladder is extended a section at a time. Some, however, are attached to the trap door, and the mere action of opening this brings the ladder down ready for use. To return the ladder, you simply reverse the process, although some models have a counterbalance to make this easier. This counterbalance may come as an optional extra, but in some cases is part of the basic ladder.

So which of the two types should you choose? The main difference is that the sectional ladder needs much more space in the loft when it is stored away than does the concertina type and if your trap door is at one end of your loft and close to a low-pitched roof you might not be able to fit it in. Most loft ladders are sold mail order and many manufacturers replying to your enquiry send out a form with a sketch on which you have to write in certain of the dimensions of your loft and landing including the ceiling height, so that they can be absolutely sure they are sending out a suitable model.

It is also true that concertina-type ladders can be fitted to smaller trap openings than can the sectional kind, but this point is not of overwhelming importance, for a small trap will not be much use to you if you intend to use your loft for storage, since it will limit the size of items that you can carry through it. In fact, enlarging the opening, in the way already described, is one of the modifications you may have to make. The other modification is changing the operation of the door so that it opens downwards. Quite what this would involve in your case, one cannot say without knowing its exact construction. Usually, however, the trap opening is lined on the underside with moulding that acts as a ledge on which a door without hinges rests, or as a stop beading for a door that opens upwards. Such moulding will have to be prised off – it is usually merely nailed in place – once the door itself has been removed. Then you re-fix the door, with the hinges arranged so that the door opens in the correct fashion (Figure 19).

The work of fitting the ladder itself involves few problems, and usually all you need do is drive in a few screws. Most manufacturers supply full and clear instructions.

For more information on loft ladders write to the manufacturers, who advertise widely in the home interest magazines.

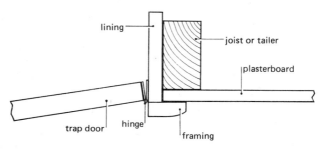

Figure 19   The trap door must be fitted to open downwards

4
The Plumbing

Your first thought on seeing the title of this chapter may well be 'What has this got to do with my plans?' and you may be tempted to skip it, thinking that it does not concern your conversion. After all, you may be saying, you do not intend to site a kitchen in your loft, are not planning a bathroom up there, do not even have it in mind to provide a washbasin in the bedrooms. So ... where's the plumbing? Well, it is almost inevitable that there will be some involved if you have the type of water system found in most British homes. For it is more than likely that right in the middle of the loft, exactly in the spot that you have allocated for your elegant new conversion, will be your cold water storage tank. If you heat your home by radiators there might even be two tanks. And the tank(s) plus all the associated pipework will have to be repositioned if you are to have enough space for your loft conversion.

Moving the cold tanks

So that you can understand all this, let me begin by explaining how typical domestic water supply works in Britain. The water enters your property via a branch line from the water board's main, which runs under the street. At the point where it does so – near the front gate, or somewhere similar – there will be a stopcock to allow you to turn it off should maintenance work ever be needed. From this point on, the system is your responsibility.

The supply pipe then passes to the house, which it will enter close by the kitchen sink. Here there will be another stopcock, to allow you to shut off the supply without having to walk down the garden path. The supply pipe will then rise up in the house, usually to the loft, and from this point on is known to plumbers as the rising main. Immediately beyond the stopcock there will be a branch line from the rising main to the cold tap at the kitchen sink, so that water used for cooking and drinking will be pure from the mains. The rising main passes up to the loft to fill the cold tank – the one that will probably be in the middle of the site for your proposed conversion.

In a few homes, however, this cold tank is not in the loft, but might be, for instance, in a cupboard on the landing. Obviously, it is then not going to interfere with your loft conversion, and you can forget about the problems I will deal with in this chapter.

The cold tank supplies cold water to all the outlets in the home other than the cold tap at the kitchen sink. It feeds all the other cold taps, the lavatory cisterns, and the hot water system. There may be slight variations from this in some homes. For instance, in some locations it might involve the use of less pipework to connect cold taps other than that at the sink direct to the rising main. Some builders do this as an economy measure – after all, copper pipe is expensive – but such practices are not common.

Water reaches the cold storage tank by virtue of pressure from the mains. When a tap is opened in the house, water from the tank flows out of it by virtue of gravity.

The entry of water into the cold tank is controlled by a ball valve. This has an arm at the end of which is a ball that used to be of metal, but in modern installations is more likely to be plastic. This ball floats on the water. When the tank is full, the ball holds the arm up high, thus shutting off the valve so that water will not enter. When water is drawn off from the tank, the water level drops, the ball falls with it, taking down the arm, and that opens the valve. Thus more water is allowed in, until the correct level is reached, which will raise the ball to a height that shuts off the valve once more. Other cisterns, such as those in lavatories, operate in exactly the same way. Of course, things can go wrong with this arrangement, and more water than is needed may be admitted to the tank, causing it to pour over the sides doing untold damage in the house below. To prevent this there is an overflow pipe, which will take excess water away, discharging it harmlessly to the garden below, and at the same time giving a warning that something is wrong.

The cold tank also feeds water to the boiler that powers the hot

water system. Most domestic hot water systems work off gravity –
but in a different way from the gravity operation of the cold tank.
Hot water is lighter than cold and in any container holding water
the hottest water will always rise to the top. So it is usual for the
boiler to be on the ground floor (in the kitchen, or behind the
living-room fire in the case of a back boiler) whilst the hot
cylinder, in which the hot water is stored ready for use, will be
sited in an airing cupboard on the first floor. Water that is heated
by the boiler passes, because it is lighter, to the hot storage
cylinder, pushing cooler water down to the boiler to be heated up
in turn. If water is drawn off from the storage cylinder, more is fed
in from the cold tank to the bottom of the hot cylinder, and this
will find its way by gravity to the boiler, to be heated up.

From the top of the hot cylinder there is another pipe, known as
the vent pipe. This passes up to the cold tank, and bends over it
rather like a shepherd's crook. The purpose of this pipe is this: if
for any reason – a faulty thermostat, for instance – the water in the
cylinder overheats, it will expand and it, plus its associated steam,
will rise up the vent pipe and be discharged harmlessly into the
cold tank. That should not put up the level in the cold tank for
almost immediately cold water will be fed from it back to the hot
cylinder. In any case, excess water can be discharged via the
overflow pipe.

A radiator system of central heating will have a similar, though
much smaller, tank, but in this case the plumbers refer to it as a
supply and expansion tank, and it is the latter word that more
accurately describes its role. The tank will have occasionally to
supply water to the heating system, for some will be lost by
evaporation, and the occasional leak. But in fact it is really an
almost empty tank to accommodate expansion of water from the
heating system as the temperature rises, and to feed it back in
when the water contracts as the temperature falls. The operation
of both water and heating systems is shown in Figure 20.

Although the type of domestic hot water system I have outlined
above is the most common, it is by no means universal. For
instance, there are locations in which every water outlet in the
house is supplied direct from the main. You usually find such
arrangements in, for example, small cottage-type houses that have
been updated. These originally will have had only one tap in the
entire house – the cold one at the kitchen sink. To keep down the

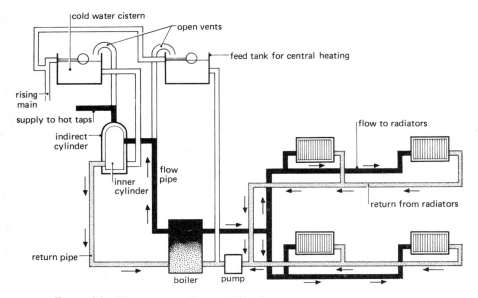

Figure 20   The water and central heating systems

costs of the modernization project, the cold taps in any new bathroom that has been installed may well have been connected direct to the main. Hot water could possibly be supplied by an instantaneous heater, which once more can have been connected direct. You find a similar set-up in large houses that have been split into flats. As a result such plumbing arrangements will not have either a cold tank or a hot storage cylinder, and the loft, if there is one, will be free of plumbing.

However, let us get back to the type of plumbing system that is more common, and certainly more likely to be found in a home in which you propose to put a room in the loft.

It is almost certain that one or both of the cold tanks will be in the way of a conversion, and they, plus their associated pipe runs, will have to be moved. In fact, if the tank is of galvanized steel, then it ought to be dispensed with, and replaced by a new one in plastic or glass fibre. Galvanized tanks have a useful life of about twenty-five years before they corrode, thus developing leaks, and have to be replaced anyway. So you might as well do the replacing now at this convenient moment, rather than at some time in the future, after your conversion is complete.

The new site

You must begin by choosing a new site for the cold tank. There are two basic possibilities. It can go to the side of your loft conversion, under the eaves of the roof, and in whatever is left of your attic after the new rooms have been built. Or it can go on top of the conversion. Both possibilities are shown in Figure 21.

In comparing the merits of the two positions, two things must be borne in mind. Firstly, you will have to include in your conversion a means of access to the tank, for even though you install a long-lasting plastic or glass fibre tank, maintenance is almost sure to be called for some day. In fact, it is almost inevitable that at some stage in the life of the tank the ball valve will need re-washering, and there may on occasion be a more serious fault than that. You have to be able to reach the tank to put things right. The access in the case of a tank under the eaves could well be a scaled-down version of a room door. For a tank in the apex of the roof, a trap door in the ceiling – like the one you probably already have into your unconverted loft – will be called for. Consider these two means of access – along with your architect if you wish – in the

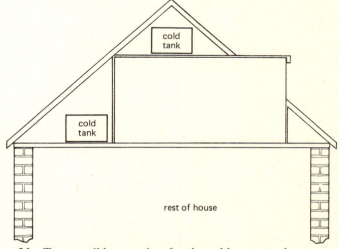

Figure 21   Two possible new sites for the cold water tank

initial planning stages, and decide which would interfere less with the ideas you have for your loft, from both the visual and practical aspects. For instance, the only possible place for a ceiling trap door might be right in the middle of your loft conversion – something that might detract from the appeal of an elegant sitting room – whilst you could fit an access door on, say, a landing or lobby at the entrance to your loft. Or it could be that the access door would have to be in a living room, while the ceiling trap could be on a landing.

The second consideration is water pressure. As it is gravity that directs water from the cold tank to the various points where it is needed, so the higher the cold tank is above the outlet the greater the pressure will be at that point. All of which means that the higher the tank, the quicker you will be able to fill, for instance, a bath, and – more important – the greater will be the spray of water at a shower rose.

So you have to take into account both these factors – access and pressure – weigh them together, and decide which of the two possibilities suits you best.

Tanks full of water are very heavy, however, and whichever spot you choose for yours, it must be well supported – what a tragedy if it were to come toppling down into your new conversion. The ceiling joists will probably be perfectly adequate – this is one of the factors your architect will have to bear in mind in deciding on their size. However, some plastic tanks are not rigid, and tend to fall out of shape under the weight of water. These need a platform underneath to prevent this.

Now let us turn for a moment to the supply and expansion tank of a central heating system. Here there is really only one consideration – means of access should anything ever go wrong, because the fact of extra water pressure is not important in this connection. However, it will almost certainly smooth the path of your plumbing operations should you position the two tanks side by side, so that is what you should aim to do.

The techniques you need

In describing the actual work, I will refer only to the main cold tank, but the procedure for dealing with both of them is basically the same, except that fewer connections are made to the heating system tank. Your first job is to empty the tank of water, and you do that by shutting off the stopcock on the rising main, and turning on one or more cold taps to draw off the water. It is a good idea, too, to turn on a hot tap to remove water from the vent pipe, but there is no need to empty the hot cylinder.

Now disconnect all the various pipes from the tank – the rising main, various feeds, and the overflow. The obvious way of doing this is to unscrew the various nuts holding them in place. If this proves difficult, however, or if the pipes are soldered in place, cut through the pipe, a short distance from the tank, and when you come to reconnect it join rerouted pipework to these short stubs of pipe. If you will be discarding the tank don't waste any time trying to undo stubborn nuts; you should always cut through the pipe to release the tank.

Cutting can be done with a hacksaw, but such a tool tends to flatten the end slightly, and that makes it difficult to obtain a watertight seal when you come to join up the pipe. It is better to use a pipe cutter. Professional plumber's cutters are expensive tools, but small ones suitable for do-it-yourself use are available. If there is not enough room to wield a pipe cutter, you will have to make do with a hacksaw, but take care to make your cuts square, and try to avoid flattening the end of the pipe.

Even though you have emptied the tanks and pipes, there will still be small amounts of water lurking in the system, and this will spill out during this operation, with the risk of damaging the ceiling below. It is as well to be ready for this, to catch such water if you can in some sort of vessel, to lay a sheet of polythene down as a protection, and to have rags ready for mopping up. Furthermore, the draw-off pipes of the cold tanks are never right at the bottom, so a residue of water will still be left in this. Take care not to spill it as you move the tank.

Site the old or replacement tank in the new position, and then connect it up properly. The rising main, supply pipes and hot cylinder vent pipe will have to be rerouted. You may be able to reroute the overflow, or you might have to fit an entirely new one.

To reroute a pipe, you will have to perform three operations; you will need to cut it, you will have to join it, and you will almost certainly be involved in bending it. This is how you carry out those operations:

Pipe cutting: I have already described how to do this in dealing with moving the old tank.

Joining pipes: The easiest way for the amateur plumber to join pipework is to use compression fittings. These come in a wide range. There is the straight coupling illustrated in Figure 22. Then there are elbow fittings to take the join round a corner, T-junctions to take a branch line off from a main run, plus couplings for joining together pipes of different sizes. All work in the same way. They consist of a body (or fitting), a coupling nut, and a small copper ring called an olive.

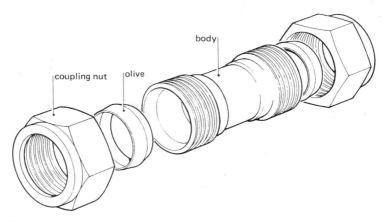

Figure 22   A compression fitting for joining pipework

To join two lengths of pipe, push the nut on to the end of the pipe, followed by the olive. If this has one chamfer longer than the other, the longer one should point towards the fitting. Push the end of the pipe into the fitting, slide the olive into the fitting, then the nut onto the threaded portion. Tighten the nut. The action of doing this will compress the olive, and you will get a watertight join. You must, however, get the tightness of the nut just right. If it is not tight enough, it will not crush the olive sufficiently to make a proper seal. If it is too tight, it will crush it so much that it will be misshapen and allow water through. Here's what you do to get things just right: turn the nut as tight as you can by hand, then take a spanner and give it one full extra turn. That should be enough. However, when you come to restore the supply of water, check each joint in turn to make sure that it is watertight. If you come across one that is weeping slightly, give the nut an extra quarter of a turn with a spanner. If it is still not leak-proof, give it another quarter turn and so on, until you are satisfied. Incidentally, a good way to test if a joint is weeping is to wipe it with paper tissue or lavatory paper. You will see at a glance if this is wet. Using your fingers is not a good idea; the skin is always moist anyway.

Any new pipe that you buy will come in metric sizes, and the ones most in use in domestic plumbing are 15, 22 and 28 mm. These are the equivalents of the old ½, ¾ and 1 in. Those metric and imperial measurements are not exact translations of each other, because in the case of metric pipe it is the external dimension that is measured, whereas the imperial diameter is the internal one. Unless your existing pipework has been installed fairly recently – say, within the past half dozen years or so – it will almost certainly be in an imperial dimension. That is not, however, an insuperable problem, for the two sizes of pipe can be connected up. Easiest of all to deal with are the 15 and 28 mm pipes, for they can be connected directly to ½ and 1 in pipes respectively. However, you are more likely to be dealing with 22 mm and ¾ in pipe, and to join these you need a special adaptor – available from plumber's merchants.

Bending pipes: The plumber uses a bending jig to bend pipes, but it is not worth your while buying one for such a small job as this, and anyway, pipe of 15 and 22 mm can be bent fairly easily by hand. Take each end of the pipe in one hand, place the centre of the bend on your knee and jerk with your hand. You will fairly easily form the curve you want. You can tie a piece of rag to your knee as protection if you wish.

The snag about this method is that you will tend to flatten the tube at the centre of the curve, and this would impede the flow of water. The way to avoid this is to use a bending spring, of a size to match the diameter of your tube. You should grease the spring first, then push it into the pipe until its centre is exactly in the middle of the proposed bend. It is better to overbend slightly at first, then bring the tube back to the required radius. When you want to remove the spring, twist it slightly to make it easier to withdraw. There is no need, incidentally, to buy a bending spring, for they can be hired.

An alternative to bending is to use elbow couplings to take the pipe round the corners. The professional plumber does not adopt this method because it is more expensive than bending, and because all joints introduce a certain amount of friction, plus the possibility of a leak, so they should be avoided if possible. However, on a comparatively small-scale job such as this, you may have so few bends to make that it would be cheaper to use the odd elbow coupling here and there than to pay the hire charges for a bending spring. Check the prices at your local plumber's merchant and hire shop to make sure.

It is just about impossible for anybody but the strong man at the circus to bend copper pipe more than 22 mm in diameter, so, if you are faced with very large pipes, you will, in any case, have to use elbow couplings.

The pipes may well have to cross joists to reach the new position of the tank. Since the pipe is rigid, it cannot, like electric cable, be passed through holes bored in the side of the joists. Instead, it will have to go in a notch, which you cut in the top of the joist, by making a couple of saw cuts and chopping out the waste with a chisel. Don't make this notch too big, for it is undesirable to cut more than necessary out of any joist in case you weaken it. But the notch must be deep enough to allow the chipboard floor to be fitted on top without damage to the pipe. You also have to beware of driving nails through these pipes when you come to fix the floor later on.

These notches constitute all the fixing the pipes will need. However, where the pipes go along the side of the joist, it is better to fix them with clips here and there.

Connecting up the tank

If you have decided on a new tank, be sure to order one of the same size as the existing one, unless your architect and/or local water board regulations stipulate a bigger one. It is as well to check this point with your local board, for new regulations may have been introduced since your water system was first designed and installed. You will have to fit at least three pipes to the tank – the rising main, one or more feeds to the rest of the house, and an overflow. A new tank will not be supplied ready-drilled with holes to receive these pipes, because the manufacturer cannot possibly know where they will be required. So place the tank temporarily in the site it will occupy, plot the runs of the various pipes, mark on the tank where the holes are to be, and drill them, preferably with a slow-speed electric drill. Your old tank will act as a guide as to how high up the side of the tank various holes should be. Note in particular that the overflow should be above the water level.

If you are re-using an existing tank, aim to make use of the existing holes, otherwise these will have to be blanked off. The expense and bother of doing this will be another factor in persuading you to dispense with an old tank, and replace it with a new one. Connections to the tank are made by means of tank connectors, which work on the compression joint principle. A ball valve will have to be fitted to the rising main connector.

In your plumbing work you might come across threaded joints. These consist of a threaded fitting – the male part of the joint – which you insert into a threaded hole, the female part, and tighten up. But this in itself does not make a watertight joint. You must use in addition PTFE tape, in conjunction with Boss White, a jointing compound, both of which are widely available at plumber's merchants. Some tradesmen use plumber's hemp instead of the tape. Here's how you make the join. The tape is wound over the male part of the thread, the Boss White is smeared on to the female thread before the male tapping is inserted into it, and tightened up. The tape should be wound tightly in the direction it will go when the joint is tightened, so that the action of your doing this does not disturb it, and should go round the threads two or three times, each turn overlapping the other. When the joint is fully tightened, a certain amount of thread should be showing. If it is not, the joint will probably not be watertight, and you should undo and remake it, this time using more tape.

This job of moving a cold tank is a highly inconvenient one for the entire household because you must shut off the water at the start of the operation, and not restore it until the job is complete. So try to do it on a day when all the family is out, or at least get them to draw off enough water for cooking and drinking purposes before you begin.

Should you be fitting a new tank, then the inconvenience will not be so great. For you can do a lot of the work – putting the new tank in position, making a lot of the connections to it – as a preliminary, before you have to turn off the water.

Your final job is to fit insulation to the tank, for your new rooms should be so well insulated that the area of the loft outside them will be a very cold place indeed, and if you leave the tank without protection you risk a freeze up.

Further reading: *The Householder's Guide to Plumbing* by James M. Haig (Stanley Paul, £3.50).

Extending the heating system

Plumbing work will also be needed if you plan to extend your present radiator system of central heating into the loft. All of the necessary work can be done yourself but, as I said in Chapter 1, you will need the advice of a heating engineer to help you plan the work.

You will have to fix the new radiators in position, run pipework to them, and connect up this pipework to the existing installation. Handling the new pipework will call once again for those techniques already required in repositioning the cold tank – i.e. cutting, joining and bending.

It is good practice to hide out of sight the pipes of a central heating installation, and the favourite place for doing this is under the floor.

It would be nice to think that you could make the pipe runs before laying the chipboard, but you cannot take pipes to a radiator until you know just where it will be, and its exact position is, really, impossible to determine until it is finally fixed to the wall. Unfortunately, though, you have to lay the floor before you build the walls. Still a lot of the preliminary work – in some cases, most of it – can be done before the chipboard decking goes down, and in the final result you might have to take up only one or perhaps two sheets. If you follow my advice (Chapter 5) about fixing the sheets with screws rather than nails, taking up and refixing the board will not present much of a problem.

Any pipes that cross the joists will, like those to and from the cold tank, have to go in notches cut in the top of the joist. If you cover the pipe at this point with lagging, it will not heat up the surrounding woodwork so much when hot water flows through it, and there will thus be less of the creaking and groaning you get with some heating systems.

The alternative to underfloor piping is to surface-mount the pipes, and you might try to plot a route for them that will mean only a short section on view in your new conversion. The pipes could then be run at skirting level, and held in place by clips. Do make sure, however, that none of your pipes are out in the cold part of what remains of your attic, unless they are lagged, for in winter they might then freeze up, with the consequent risk of a burst that would send water cascading down into the rest of your home.

Where a pipe has to pass through a ceiling or floor you make the holes for this with the normal carpentry tools of brace and bit, or drill and bit.

Now ... where are you going to fix your new radiators? Normally, whenever possible, they are sited under a window, and with a simple dormer this is feasible. However, if you have floor-to-ceiling dormer windows, then obviously, a radiator cannot be placed under them. Nevertheless, it is always a good idea to site it somewhere near the window, for not only is this normally the coldest part of the room, but also the pane of glass constitutes a large cold panel, the very existence of which sets up movements of cold air, that for all the world feel like the chilling draughts caused by wind whistling through gaps round the frame. A nearby radiator can warm up the glass and help to stop those down-draughts as they are known.

A radiator has to be assembled before you can fix it (Figure 23). At each of the four corners you will find a threaded hole. One of the top ones takes the air vent, with which you bleed out any air that gets into the radiator when the system is working; the other is merely blanked off to make it watertight. It does not matter which goes where, so fix the vent into the hole that will be most easily accessible when the radiator is in position. The two bottom holes take the valves. The wheel valve, or hand control as it is sometimes called, which you use to shut down the radiator when you do not want it in use, goes at one side and the lockshield valve, which is used for adjusting the flow of water, goes to the other. All four items are fitted by means of threaded joints, which I have described earlier in this chapter.

When fitting the blanking-off plug into the radiator it can be difficult to get a sufficient grip to tighten it up properly. Plumbers have a bar that they push into the hole of the plug, and they get extra leverage if needed by gripping this bar with a movable

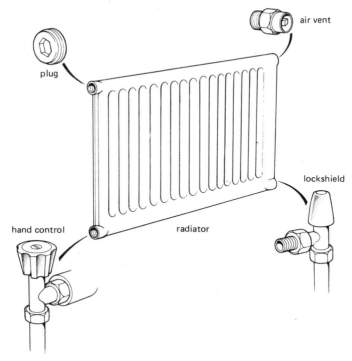

Figure 23   Assembling a radiator

spanner or wrench. If you do not have a bar, you might get away with a large screwdriver, the blade of which you insert into the hole, its tip engaging diagonally in two corners.

At the opposite corner goes the air vent. Some types of vent consist of two parts – the vent itself and a plug into which the vent is inserted. Unscrew the vent from the plug, fix the plug in the radiator using a threaded joint and tighten it, once again using a bar or a screwdriver. Then insert the vent in the plug, without using tape or Boss White, and tighten it up with the vent key, the tool that is used for bleeding the radiator. Should you get a vent that is fixed in its plug, use this key for the whole tightening operation.

The valves, too, come in two parts – the valve itself and the radiator insert – although they will probably be loosely threaded together when you get them. The radiator insert is a male fitting that is threaded into the female tapping of the radiator itself. Then the male main body of the valve is fixed into the insert. In both cases, use a threaded joint.

Once the radiator is assembled in this way, it can be fixed to the wall. Details vary between different makes, but basically, you screw a couple of brackets to the wall, and the radiator is then 'hung' on these brackets by means of two fixing lugs on its back. It is important, however, to take some trouble over positioning the radiator, because it can look comical if not sensibly aligned. For instance, it should be placed centrally on the window. It is quite easy to do this. Determine the centre point of the window opening, and mark it in pencil on the wall below. Use a plumb line and bob to mark a vertical line here. Measure the distance between the centre point of the two fixing lugs on the back of the radiator, and divide that measurement by two. The two brackets should be fixed each side of the centre line on the wall, and the distance of that half measurement away from it. The radiator should also be truly horizontal, although a slight slope up towards the air vent is not a bad idea, so that you can bleed out air more effectively. Use a spirit level to ensure that the brackets are fixed at the same height.

You do not, of course, have to go to such trouble when the radiator is not under a window, but even so you should try to make it level, and align it sensibly with any nearby architectural feature, so that it does not look out of true.

What height should the radiator be from the floor? If the pipes feeding it are to come up through the floorboards it does not really matter, although a radiator under a window will look better if it is slightly nearer to the sill than to the floor. But if the pipes are to run along the wall or skirting below you must leave enough room for them to bend up towards it. If there is not much room, you will take up less space by using an elbow coupling, instead of bending the pipe, and you will then need about 88 mm ($3\frac{1}{2}$ in) between the floor and the bottom of the radiator.

You often find that one of the fixing holes in the brackets is an elongated slot rather than a round hole. In that case fix the bracket initially just through the slot, hang the radiator in place, and check to see that it looks all right. Remove the radiator, make any adjustments necessary in the positioning of the brackets, and complete the fixing by driving screws through the remaining round holes.

Incidentally, a radiator full of water is a very heavy object, and so the brackets need to be firmly fixed in place. This is definitely one of those objects for which special frame members need to be inserted during the construction of a wall (see section on building a wall in Chapter 6).

When the installation of your radiator(s) is complete, run pipe from it to the point at which your heating engineer advises it should join up to the main system. The connection of the pipe to the valves of the radiator is by means of a compression joint. Your engineer will tell you what size of tube to use, but it is likely to be 22 mm.

The connection of the new pipe to the existing installation will also be by means of a compression joint, and you will probably use a T-fitting for this. First, though, the system will have to be drained off, or at least that part of it that is higher up than the point at which you will be making the joint, otherwise water will flow out when you cut into the pipe.

To empty water from the system, look for the draincock. There is bound to be one somewhere, and it will be down near the lowest point of the installation. To this draincock, fix a length of hosepipe, which should be run to a drain somewhere. Shut off the water to the supply and expansion tank. You can do this by closing down the stop tap on the rising main, but this will deprive the whole house of water. Should you want to avoid this inconvenience you can do so by placing a stick across the top of the supply and expansion tank, and tying the arm of the ball valve to it. That will mean the ball cannot fall as the water level does, and so cannot turn on the supply. Open the draincock.

With the draining complete, insert a T joint in the correct spot in the system, and connect up the new pipes to this. Restore the water supply and test that the joint is watertight. Turn on the heating, and check that heat is reaching the new radiators. When the system is fully operational, all the radiators should be at the same temperature. If not, adjustments can be made by opening the lockshield valve further to cool down the radiator, or closing it slightly to warm it up.

I deal more fully with what is involved in installing central heating systems in my book *Home Heating and Fireplaces: a Do-It-Yourself Guide* (Stanley Paul, £1.75).

5
The Floor

Your loft extension will need to have what is known in the jargon of builders as a suspended timber floor. This consists of a timber surface on top of, and fixed to, a network of joists.

You will more than likely have such a floor in your house at present, at least in the upper storey, if not on the ground floor. But, unless your home was built in the last ten years or so, your suspended timber floor will probably be surfaced with floorboards. However, the soaring cost of timber has made floorboards a very uneconomic proposition indeed, and, increasingly, builders are making use of chipboard, which can cost up to 30 per cent less. I would advise you to do the same in your loft conversion, for I think you will find this material easier to handle, as well as being cheaper. Moreover, it forms a smooth surface on which all types of floor covering can be laid. But please note that you must use the correct grade of chipboard.

With the introduction of British Standard 5669 in 1979, four different types of chipboard are now defined. These are: Type I – standard; Type II – flooring; Type III – improved moisture resistant; Type II/III – flooring, with improved moisture resistance. Only boards of Type II or II/III should be used. A good timber merchant will know what you are talking about if you quote these types to him.

The floor should be laid quite early on in the construction work – although see my remarks about running electric cables (Chapter 7) – for, with the floor in position, you have something on which you can actually walk, instead of having to balance precariously on joists. The floor will, in any event, have to be fixed before the walls, for the base of these will actually rest on the floor.

The floor will be one of the parts of your conversion that your architect will specify in detail, but let us look at some of the factors to be taken into consideration.

One of the first problems will be deciding if the existing joists are strong enough. Remember that in the first place they were designed merely to carry the top-floor ceiling, which will have been fixed to their undersides. Now not only do they have to carry the weight of your room in the loft itself, but also they might have to carry new roof supports, inserted to compensate for those you removed to clear a big enough space in the middle of the attic. Are they strong enough? Almost certainly the answer will be No, but only an expert can decide.

The strengthening, if this is felt necessary, may well consist of new, bigger joists being fixed to the existing ones. It could prove impossible to take up into the restricted space inside the loft, joists big enough to cover the entire span, and two half-length joists may well have to be used instead.

Or your architect might decide on totally new joists, resting on the front and back external walls of your house, and supported intermediately on internal load-bearing walls. He might even feel that the construction needs to be strengthened with steel beams.

Manoeuvring the joists into the attic can present quite a problem, and probably the best time to take them up there is when a hole has been made in the roof to allow the dormer window or windows to be inserted. Some form of hoist may well be needed.

So you can see that this is a very complicated business, and you might well feel that the strengthening of the joists is something that should be left to a builder.

Now let's move on to the actual flooring material – the chipboard. Flooring quality chipboard comes with three different shapes on its sides – or edge profiles, to use a more technical term. The sheets can be tongued and grooved, rather like floorboards, on two sides or four; they can have loose tongues; or they can have straight sides, the correct term for this latter being square edged. All three are shown in Figure 24.

Flooring chipboard is also available in two main thicknesses – 18 mm ($\frac{3}{4}$ in) or 22 mm ($\frac{7}{8}$ in). The latter sheets will obviously be more expensive, and heavier, but do not need so many joists to

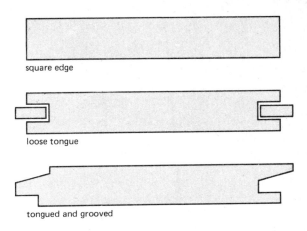

square edge

loose tongue

tongued and grooved

Figure 24   The three different edge profiles of flooring quality chipboard

support them, for they can be more widely spaced. So it is up to your architect to work out which would be most economical for you, bearing in mind the spacing of the ceiling joists you have at present. It could well be, to quote an example, that you could get away with this present spacing if you use 22 mm thick chipboard, but you would need to insert extra ones if you were to settle for 18 mm thick material. Recommended spacings for joists are a maximum of 450 mm (about 18 in) between centres for 18 mm chipboard, and 610 mm (about 24 in) for the 22 mm variety. However, the inner London bylaws call for 400 mm and 600 mm respectively between centres.

The chipboard is also available in various sheet sizes – 2440×1220 mm (8×4 ft) and 2440×600 mm (8×2 ft) being the most common. The larger boards would make for speedier installation ... by a trained operator. Because such boards are more unwieldy and heavier to carry, a do-it-yourselfer might make quicker progress with the smaller ones. However, you would experience no difficulty in lifting the larger sheets, if you have a helper.

Tradesmen usually fix the boards with nails, but all the hammering that this involves might cause vibrations that would harm the ceiling below, and you might think it worth the extra expense of screws instead. The screws to use are 2 in No. 8 countersunk. These will be much cheaper if you order them in bulk – in boxes of 100 or even 200. Using screws instead of nails also involves you in extra work, as well as expense, but if you use a power tool to drill clearance holes in the chipboard for the screw shank, then drive the screws home with a push-pull, spiral ratchet screwdriver, the extra labour should not be too arduous. The recommendation with nails, incidentally, is that they should be punched 2–3 mm ($\frac{1}{8}$ in) below the surface of the board. A spiral ratchet screwdriver should easily drive screws that far below the surface of the board, without any need for a countersunk hole. Anyway, let us take a look at how you construct a floor.

First, do you have any insulation in your loft? If you do, it would be a good idea to remove it from that part of the loft that will be under the rooms your conversion will create. You see, heat rises, and warmth coming up from the rest of the house will help to give your loft extension more comfortable temperatures – always providing there is no barrier of insulating material. But the area of your present loft that will lie outside the finished extension needs to retain its insulation in order to stop heat leaking out from the rooms below. In fact, it might need extra insulation for, due to soaring fuel costs, we have in recent years revised our ideas on how much insulation is desirable. At one time a 25 mm (1 in) layer was thought sufficient, but nowadays 100 mm (4 in) is the recommendation, especially if you have central heating. So don't throw away the insulation you take up from under your new rooms. It could well go to giving you a better standard of insulation in the attic area outside the conversion.

If your loft has no insulation at present, you should provide it in these latter areas. But first enquire about the possibilities of a grant (see Chapter 1).

Next, how much of the loft are you going to cover with chipboard decking? Your floor will have to stretch to at least the full external dimension of your room – i.e. to the outside of its walls – but you may want to extend the flooring beyond the limits of your conversion, both to give easy access to the plumbing and any other services located up there should maintenance ever be needed in future, and also to provide extra storage space. For those parts of your loft that do not – or for various reasons cannot – form part of the habitable conversion can still be put to good use as a sort of junk room. If you do extend the flooring make sure you include in the walls of your conversion an access door to the loft areas beyond. This need not, of course, be a full-size door such as you need for access to the room itself.

When your chipboard arrives, it must be stored properly until you are ready to use it. It should be stacked flat, and off the ground, and sheltered from the weather. Bad storage can cause permanent distortion of the boards, and so should be avoided at all costs. Make sure you have somewhere ready to receive them when they are delivered. Do not, however, take them straight from store to fix them. It is a good idea to loose-lay the boards in the attic for at least 24 hours before you fix them, in order to condition them, as joiners say. This allows them to adjust to the moisture conditions of your attic – and swell or shrink, as need be.

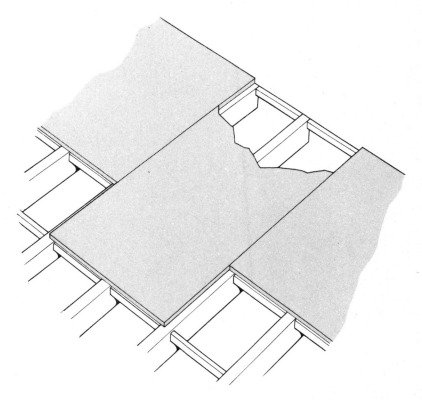

Figure 25 With square edged boards, the long edges should fall along the centre of the joists

Square edged boards need to be supported all the way round their perimeter. The long edges should fall on the centre of the joists – so make sure you match up the spacing of the joists with the width of the boards – and their short edges should be fixed to 38 mm (1½ in) wide noggings, the ends of which have been secured to the joists (Figure 25). Screws or nails should be 200–300 mm (8–12 in) apart round the edges, 400–500 mm (16–20 in) apart on intermediate joists, and should be about 9 mm (⅓ in) from the edge of the board.

Tongued and grooved boards go with the long edges across the joists (Figure 26). They must, however, be supported at the ends, so the short edges must fall in the middle of the joist – they should not cantilever. There should be four fixings to each joist – one

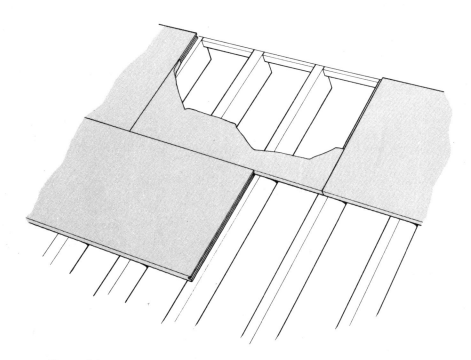

Figure 26   Tongued and grooved boards should be fixed with the long edges across the joists

25 mm (1 in) in from each edge of the board, and the others spaced equidistantly between.

With both types of board, you get a stronger result if you glue the edges, using a PVA woodworking adhesive.

Both types of board should be laid with the cross joints staggered (see Figures 25 and 26). Here's how you ensure that. When you come to the end of a row, you will, inevitably, have to cut a board to a length to fit the space left. Do not throw the waste away, but use it to start off the next row. Automatically, this will stagger the joints; should the waste be impossibly small – or indeed in the rare event of your being able to make up a floor from whole boards – then use a board sawn in half to start off the second row.

The edges should be tightly butted up against each other. However, if the edges of the floor round the perimeter of the whole butt up against a wall, or something similar, you must leave an expansion gap. This gap needs to be 2 mm for every metre of the run of the floor, with 10 mm being regarded as a minimum. If you want an imperial translation of those dimensions, they work out to about $\frac{1}{12}$ in for every $39\frac{1}{2}$ in of floor, with $\frac{2}{5}$ in being regarded as a minimum. In an attic conversion it is, of course, more likely that the walls will stand on the floor.

With a chipboard floor, it is possible to form a trap that will allow you to reach any services that may require attention in the future – electric cable, for instance. Make sure that the trap is supported on all four edges by joists and/or noggings. It should be fixed with 2 in No. 8 countersunk screws – even a tradesman would not use nails for this since it would be very difficult to lever them out when you wanted to raise the trap.

Your chipboard floor is suitable for all types of floor covering, and both sheets and tiles can be bonded directly to it with most normal floorlaying adhesives. However, if a water-based adhesive with a high water content is to be used, the floor should be sealed with a polyurethane lacquer first. With no floor covering whatsoever, except perhaps for a few rugs scattered here and there, a sealed chipboard floor is highly attractive in its own right.

For further information contact The Chipboard Promotion Association Ltd, 7a Church Street, Esher, Surrey KT10 8QS. Telephone Esher 66468/9.

6
Building the Shell

Once the floor has been installed and the windows have been fitted, you can set about creating the shell of your room or rooms, by building the walls and ceiling. The best material to use for this is undoubtedly plasterboard. This meets the fire-risk provisions of the Building Regulations (or as your architect would be more likely to phrase it, the spread-of-flame requirements), is an easy material for the do-it-yourselfer to handle, and requires the minimum of tools. You should have no difficulty whatsoever in getting a very professional finish, especially if you use tapered edge board (Figure 27) and follow the method outlined later on for dealing with the joints between the sheets.

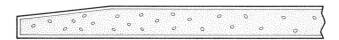

Figure 27   Tapered edge plasterboard

But that's not all. Insulation is a vital part of your conversion. Stuck up high in the roof of your house, your loft extension will be occupying an exposed spot, and be much more vulnerable to the weather than the existing rooms lower down in the house. Unless you insulate it to high standards, your attic will be a very cold place indeed. And it's not just a matter of heat insulation. A loft is not only a cold place; it is also a noisy one, with the spattering of raindrops on the tiles, the running of water down gutters, the sound of adjacent plumbing, and the twittering of birds on the roof. The materials that stop heat escaping from your home also offer a fair degree of sound insulation, and will make your extension a quieter place.

One of the advantages of plasterboard is that you can buy it with insulating material bonded to the back. For example, Gyproc urethane laminate has a backing of paper-faced rigid polyurethane foam that is either 13 mm ($\frac{1}{2}$ in) or 20 mm ($\frac{3}{4}$ in) thick. The latter, in particular, offers a very high degree of insulation.

Plasterboard that is insulated in this manner should, of course, be used only on the ceiling and the external walls of your conversion – i.e. those that divide it from the roof space, or the house next door. Walls that are acting merely as a partition between two or more rooms in your loft can be built of ordinary plasterboard. This type of board can, of course, be used on any of the walls, providing you add some form of insulation.

Plasterboard is a very heavy material, and you will certainly need a helper to lift it, especially when dealing with the ceiling. The board comes in sheets 1200 mm (47$\frac{1}{4}$ in) wide and either 1800 mm (about 71 in) or 2400 mm (94$\frac{1}{2}$ in) long. On ceilings it might be as well for you to use the smaller ones, since you will undoubtedly find these easier to handle. You will almost certainly need the 2400 mm sheets for the walls in order to meet the required height of your room. The material is available in two thicknesses – 9.5 mm (about $\frac{3}{8}$ in) and 12.7 mm (approximately $\frac{1}{2}$ in). The thicker board is a lot heavier, and also more expensive. However, it needs fewer timber supports, and so, given the price of timber today, it could in the long run work out much cheaper to use it. As for the extra weight, two reasonably agile men should have no difficulty whatsoever in handling a 12.7 mm thick sheet.

One other point: throughout your loft conversion it would be as well to incorporate a vapour check to stop condensation getting through and soaking the insulation material beyond, for this would render it ineffective. A new product called Gyproc wall coat will do this. Apply two coats by brush or roller to the face of the board, and, as well as getting the vapour check, you also are priming and sealing the board to make decoration easier, and making the job of hiding the joints simpler. The product is available where you buy plasterboard.

Gyproc urethane laminate is also 1200 mm (47$\frac{1}{4}$ in) wide, but it comes in three lengths – 2400 mm (94½ in), 2438 mm (96 in), and 2700 mm (106¼ in). It incorporates its own vapour check. However, you can create a complete vapour barrier by treating it with Gyproc wall coat.

Working with plasterboard

Plasterboard is a very easy material to work with, but you need to handle it carefully. For instance, you must be ready to receive it properly when it is delivered. It should be carried on edge – you will need a helper for this – and should be stored flat (otherwise it might buckle, and be difficult to fix) in a dry place. So be sure you allocate a proper space for this. The manufacturers recommend that the stacks of the material should not exceed 900 mm (3 ft).

The material has an ivory coloured face. It should always be fixed with this side outwards, and be cut etc. from the ivory side, too. You will see at a glance which way a board with insulation added should be fixed.

You cut plasterboard to size with much the same sort of saw you use on timber-based boards, provided this is fine toothed and sharp. However, you can take off a short length by scoring deeply with a sharp knife – a Stanley knife is ideal – snapping the board over a straight edge, and cutting through the paper backing.

If you need to cut a hole in the middle of a panel – as you will to take electric fittings, for instance – draw its outline on the face in pencil, drill a starting hole with either a hand or electric drill, using an ordinary twist bit, at each corner, insert a thin-bladed saw in each starting hole in turn, and saw out the required shape.

Always lightly sand all cut edges with a fine glasspaper before fixing the board.

The plasterboard is normally fixed to its timber framework with special galvanized plasterboard nails. These should be driven in straight with a carpenter's hammer, until the head slightly dimples the surface of the board, but without fracturing the paper liner. However, as I have said elsewhere, doing a lot of hammering in an attic is not always to be recommended to the do-it-yourselfer, and it might be as well if you were to use No. 6 galvanized screws instead. These should be 38 mm (1½ in) long. On urethane laminate, they should be 25 mm (1 in) longer than the thickness of the material. You will have to drill a clearance hole for the screws in the plasterboard.

You will get a slight gap between the edges of the boards, and at corners, but it is much easier than you might think to disguise them. You do so with filling material and tape, applied with special tools – an applicator, taping knife and jointing sponge. All are available where you buy the plasterboard. The technique consists of applying the filler, then pressing the tape into it, and covering with more filler. But full instructions are available from the supplier.

When a professional uses this method, you would find it totally impossible to see where the joints have been after decoration. And there is no doubt that, provided you take care, you can achieve pretty impressive results, too. A thick, heavy wallpaper, for instance, would hide most imperfections.

The filling material is also used for covering nail and screw heads. This operation is carried out in two parts. First you put on a thin coat of joint filler over the head, then one of joint finish.

For external corners, a special corner tape, incorporating two parallel metal strips, reinforces the angle, and gives a clean sharp edge. Full instructions are, once again, supplied.

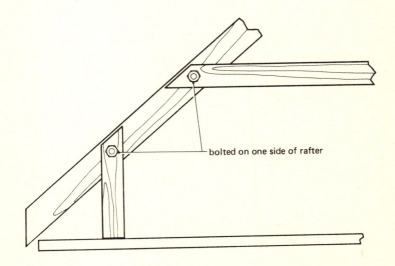

bolted on one side of rafter

Figure 28   A simple method of fixing joists for the new ceiling

The ceiling

Your first job will be to install a network of joists to which the new ceiling can be fixed. Your architect will detail a method of fixing for these, but one he may well recommend is shown in Figure 28.

Here a ceiling joist, consisting of unplaned timber, is fixed at each end to the existing rafters of the roof. The size of the joist will depend on its span – follow your architect's advice on this. There is no need for any joint where the timbers meet – the new ceiling joist can merely lie on the face of the rafter. The method of fixing favoured by most tradesmen would probably be to use large nails. But once again, to avoid disturbing loose tiles on the roof, it would probably be better to choose some other method. A nut and bolt

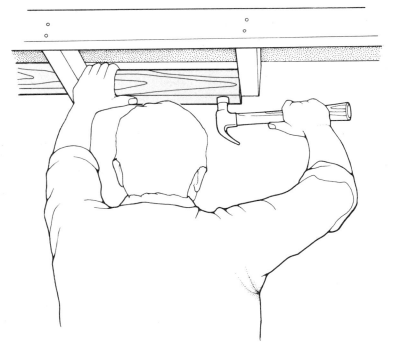

Figure 29   Noggings should be inserted so that all edges of each plasterboard sheet are supported

would be a good idea. Figure 28 shows the construction at its simplest; the whole thing could be complicated by the insertion of a dormer window into the roof.

With the joists in place, you can begin to fix the plasterboard. For joists spaced at centres up to 450 mm (17¾ in) you can use 9.5 mm (⅜ in) thick material, but if they are wider apart than that, and up to 600 mm (23⅜ in), use the thicker 12.7 mm (½ in) board. Joists spaced at 600 mm (23⅜ in) are also suitable for urethane laminate.

The plasterboard should be fixed across the joists, and the ends should ideally coincide with the centre of a joist. Noggings should be fixed along the sides of the board, so that the sheet is supported on all edges (Figure 29). Fixings should be at 150 mm (6 in) centres, and no closer than 13 mm (½ in) to the edge.

Begin in one corner of the room. With your helper hoist the board up to the joists, and start the fixing. You will find it much easier to work from a scaffold board supported at each end, rather than have each of you standing on a separate pair of household steps. But whatever you stand on, take great care to ensure that you do not fall off, causing yourself an injury.

The usual method of work is for one man to use both his hands and the top of his head to hold the board in the correct position. The other can also offer support by balancing the board on his head, whilst he starts the fixing. When enough fixings have been made to allow the board to stay securely in place both can withdraw their support and carry on with the fixing.

Once the first board is in place, the next one to it can be fixed, leaving a gap of about 3 mm (⅛ in) between the ends. Eventually, you will come to the end of a row, and have to cut a board to fit. Start the next row with the waste piece cut from this board just as when you are laying a chipboard floor (see previous chapter), so that the cut ends will be staggered (Figure 30). This is known as 'breaking the bond' in the parlance of the trade. In the unlikely event of you finding that an exact number of uncut boards equals the span of the ceiling, you will have to cut a board in half to start the next row, in order to make sure that you break the bond.

Bound edges of Gyproc urethane laminate should be butted together and fixed not closer than 10 mm (⅜ in) to the edge. Cut ends should be fixed not closer than 13 mm (½ in) to the edges. Fixings should be at 230 mm (9 in) centres.

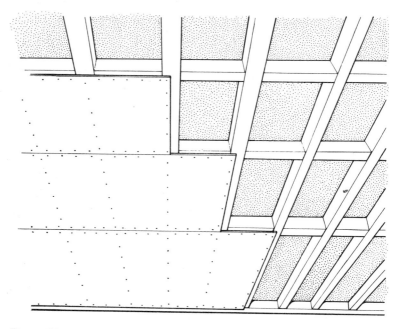

Figure 30   Cut ends of plasterboard ceiling staggered and centred over a support

Hollow-joisted ceilings

In the foregoing section I assumed that you would be constructing a conventional ceiling. You might, however, in order to get extra headroom, be installing a hollow-joisted one, with the plasterboard fixed on top, rather than to the bottom, of the joists. In many ways this will be easier, provided you have enough room on top of the joists in which to work. You and your helper merely hoist the board up into its correct position, then fix it with screws at your leisure, without needing to hold it in position.

In some locations, once the ceiling joists have been erected, there simply may not be enough space to allow you to hoist large sheets of plasterboard on top of the joists. Take stock of your attic before you begin, to see if you will be faced with such a situation. Should you find you will be, here's what to do. Fit joists to half, or perhaps even three quarters of the room, then take enough sheets of plasterboard to span the whole room, and store them on top of the joists. When the time comes to fix the ceiling you merely slide each sheet of board into its correct position and fix it.

A trap in the ceiling

If you are siting a cold water tank in the apex of the roof and above your loft conversion (see Chapter 4) you will have to make an access trap in the ceiling so that you can get at the tank and its associated pipework should that ever be necessary. Right from the moment you plan the ceiling, you must make provision for such a trap. Your architect will detail the construction, but this is one method that he might well follow. The work should, of course be done before the sheets of plasterboard are fixed.

It is unlikely that the new ceiling joists will be spaced far enough apart to allow enough space for the trap, so one or more joists that

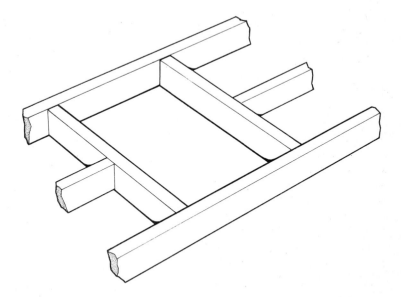

Figure 31   Construction of the opening for a trap in the new ceiling for access to the cold water tank

lie across the middle of the proposed opening will have to be cut.
The ends cannot be left flapping free, however, and each of them is
fixed to a cross member that in turn is fixed to the joist on each
side. These cross members are known as trimmers, and they
should be of the same size as the joists themselves. In fact, the
waste from the joist you have to cut might well serve as one
trimmer. The construction is shown in Figure 31.

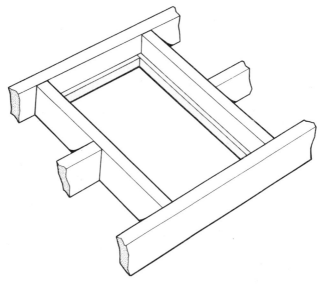

Figure 32   Construction of a trap door in the new ceiling

These trimmers form the basic shape of the trap, but the
opening does need to be lined so that it will not be an eyesore.
Before we go on to that, however, we first have to consider how
you are going to climb through the opening. This is important
because, as you will have seen in Chapter 3, which deals with the
means of access to your loft, if you propose to fit a loft ladder, then
the trap door has to open downwards, although ceiling trap doors
normally open upwards. So if you do decide on a loft ladder, hinge
the door the correct way from the start.

I am going, however, to take the optimistic view that very little is
ever going to go wrong with your cold tank, that you will seldom

need to gain access to it, and thus the expense of a loft ladder to make entry easy would be a waste of money. Accordingly I suggest the simple construction shown in Figure 32. To the sides of the joists and trimmers fix lengths of timber about 50×25 mm (2×1 in). This can be timber that is square edged on all sides, or you can choose wood with a decorative moulding on the lower edge. This timber should be positioned so that its lower edge will at least come level with the face of the plasterboard, once that is fixed, and indeed, if you are going to err at all it is better that the timber protrudes slightly, rather than that it should fall short. The join between the plasterboard and timber should be treated in the same way as joins between sheets of board. The timber will form a ledge, and your door can merely rest on this – there is no need for any hingeing. The door, which can be a plain sheet of blockboard, should be of such a size that it is big enough to rest on the ledge but not so big that it is too tight a fit in the opening. To open it, you merely push it gently upwards, and lower it into position when you want to close it. Make sure that the opening is well covered with insulating material, and, when you disturb this in order to gain access, take care to rearrange it properly.

The walls

With the ceiling securely in position, you can start to build the walls. Here is a good method of building a non-load-bearing partition – i.e. a wall that is merely dividing up space, and is playing no part in holding anything up (Figure 33). Once again you use plasterboard, this time fixed to a framework of 75×50 mm (3×2 in) unplaned softwood.

Begin by marking out in pencil on the floor the outline of the walls. Make corresponding pencil lines on the ceiling, using a plumb line and bob to ensure that these lines are exactly above those on the floor.

Fix a length of the timber along the line on the floor – this is known as sole plate, and should be one continuous piece, except where there is to be a door in the wall. The sole plate should be nailed (or better still, bearing in mind my remarks elsewhere about excessive vibration, screwed) to the floor below at 200 mm (8 in) centres in the case of a plate running parallel to the joists. A plate that runs across the joists should be fixed to each joist.

A corresponding length of timber – known as the head plate – should now be fixed to the ceiling. Screwing this to the plaster-board simply will not do. The screws must go through to the joists or noggings above. If there are none, noggings will have to be inserted specially. This fact may here and there cause you to revise your plans, and slightly alter the position of a wall so that it lies directly below a joist.

Now you must fix a series of vertical studs (lengths of timber) between the two plates. You need one at each end of the wall and, measuring from one end, in between at 400 mm ($15\frac{3}{4}$ in) centres for 9.5 mm thick board, or 600 mm ($23\frac{1}{2}$ in) centres for the

Figure 33   Building a non-load-bearing partition wall

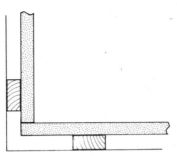

Figure 34   An internal angle in the wall

12.7 mm thick material and Gyproc urethane laminate. The last stud will be nearer to the end upright than those recommended spacings. Follow these measurements accurately, for they are necessary not only to give the wall proper support, but also they match up to the widths of the plasterboard. Undoubtedly, you will not be able to make up your wall from a set of complete boards, but will have to cut one at the end to a width to fit. But, if, working from one end, you have placed the studs at the correct spacing, the last stud at the opposite end will be in the correct position to receive the cut board.

You must measure and cut each stud individually to the right length, and fix it in position to both the head and sole plates with a screw driven in at an angle from each side into the plate below or above. In addition to the vertical studs, noggings are needed

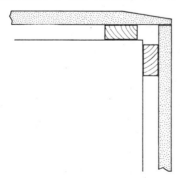

Figure 35   An external angle in the wall

halfway up the wall, and these should be fixed to the verticals in the same way. If you think you will want to fix any heavy items of equipment – built-in furniture, for instance – to the wall, determine its position in advance and place extra studs or noggings in the right place to receive the fixing screws after the wall is complete.

Now let us come back to a wall in which there will be a door. In this wall, the head plate should still be continuous, but obviously the sole plate needs to be broken for the door. You would do well to buy a standard door, rather than think of making one, and you should leave a gap big enough for this door and its frame. You will, of course, require a vertical stud at each side of the door opening and a nogging at the top of the door opening.

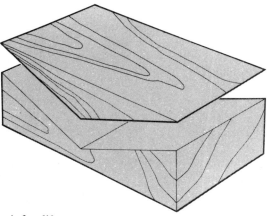

Figure 36   A footlifter

You will get two types of angle in your walls – internal and external. The former occur at the normal corners of the room, whilst you may well get the latter where the opening for a dormer joins up with the main walls, or at a 'reveal' for a door. The framework for both is shown in the figures – an internal angle in Figure 34 and an external in Figure 35.

When the frame is finished, you can fix the plasterboard to it. Cut the boards 25 mm (1 in) less than the height of the wall, press them tight against the ceiling, and fix in place. It is not a bad idea to improvise a footlifter, as shown in Figure 36, to allow you easily to raise the board to the correct position. The board should be fixed to each and every member of the frame at 150 mm (6 in) centres, and the nails or screws should be no closer than 13 mm (½ in) to the edge of each board. The boards should be butted against each other along the edges.

Should the wall be dividing two rooms, it will need to have plasterboard fixed to both sides and, if you use the 12.7 mm thick board, you will have a fairly high standard of sound insulation – enough for two bedrooms, for example. But if you want a higher degree – because, say, one room is to be a teenager's den, whilst the other may be intended as a study – fit two layers of plasterboard to each side. The vertical joins of these boards should be staggered, but all edges need to be nailed to a stud. If in addition you fill the gap between with insulating material, or use an insulation-backed plasterboard, you will have a very effective noise barrier indeed.

Because you are unused to dealing with plasterboard, you might get a slight gap where the wall meets the ceiling, and whilst this will be barely noticeable to anyone else who looks at it, its existence will bother you. You could fill such a gap, before you decorate, with some form of stopper, such as cellulose filler. But a much better idea might well be to disguise any imperfections by fitting a plaster-based cove at the angle (Figure 37). In any event, such a cove forms a nice detail, even where the join between the walls and ceiling is perfect. The cove to use is composed of a fire-resistant plaster core, encased in a paper liner, and you can fix it to the plasterboard of walls and ceiling with a powdered adhesive, which you mix with water.

The cove is easily cut to length with any fine-toothed saw. It has to be mitred at corners, but templates, to ensure that you cut these accurately, are supplied and furthermore the adhesive can also be used as a filler to mask any bad joins. Full instructions are supplied when you buy the cove.

Cladding brick walls

In many conversions it could happen that one of the brick walls of the house is used as an actual wall of the new room in your loft. Referring to the sample houses in Figure 11 (page 21), you will see that this could be true of both end walls of the terraced house, the dividing wall between the two semis, and the end wall of any

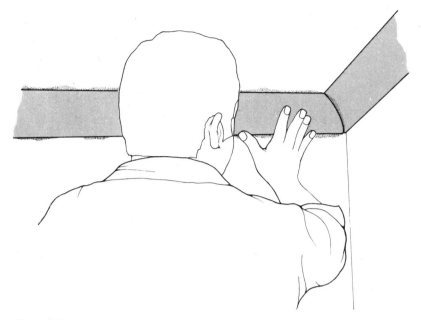

Figure 37   A cove can be used to cover the gap where the wall meets
the ceiling

house where the roof is not hipped. But you ought to ponder
before you take this opportunity, because there is a risk that your
loft extension would not be as well insulated as it ought to be. Let
me explain how this could happen.

The brick wall will, of course, need to be covered in some way,
before it can form part of your new room. You may wonder
whether this is necessarily so, bearing in mind that unconcealed
brickwork is used as a feature wall in many ultra-modern homes.
But brickwork of that type has to be designed right from the start
to be on display. The bricks have to be laid and the mortar
trimmed, with special care – fair face brickwork is the way the
bricklayers themselves describe it. Any old brickwork will not do.
Certainly one can say, without fear of contradiction, that the
brickwork inside your loft will not be good enough to form a
feature wall in an elegant room.

So, what to cover it with? A builder would probably opt for
plaster. But plastering is just about the most skilled of all the

building trades, and there is no doubt that it is out of the question for any do-it-yourselfer to get a professional-looking result with plaster.

Fortunately, there is an alternative, and that is to clad the wall with plasterboard. The method for doing this is to screw a framework of 50×25 mm (2×1 in) battens to the wall, and fix the plasterboard to this, in pretty much the same way that you apply the plasterboard of a partition wall to the timber studs.

But first it is a good idea to take a look at that wall and ask exactly what it consists of. If it is the external wall of a modern house, it will certainly be of cavity construction, and if you clad it with plasterboard then the insulation standards of your loft conversion will be up to those of the rest of the house. In fact, slightly better, because the space between plasterboard and brick-work will add its own extra insulation. If the brick wall is an outside one of a somewhat older house, and is a solid wall, the situation might not be too bad, provided that the wall is well built, and is in sound condition. After all a combination of the wall, a 25 mm gap filled with insulation, and the plasterboard, adds up to a fair amount of protection, although I would not blame anyone who wanted higher standards. But if the wall is merely the sort of thin partition that you often find dividing the lofts of adjacent terraced houses or paired semis, then you will want something better in the way of insulation. After all, on the other side of that thin wall is your neighbour's loft. If he has insulated it well – as he will have done if he has any sense – then it is going to be a very cold place indeed. You need a lot of insulation to keep at bay the cold coming from it – and the noise of any cold water tank, and other bits of the plumbing system, that happen to be up there.

In such a situation – and, indeed, any other where you want a high standard of insulation – you should use a plasterboard that incorporates insulating material.

Anyway, this is a good method for cladding a brick wall with plasterboard (Figure 38). First screw a framework of battens to the wall. Beware of doing this in a slapdash fashion, otherwise when you come to fix the plasterboard to the battens, it will not form a smooth, attractive surface; instead you will have a wall that is undulating and full of ripples. So although it involves a fair bit of trouble, it is worth while taking care over the fixing of the battens to ensure that you get a first-class job. Here's what you do.

The main problem lies in the fact that the wall will not present a true flat surface all the way along its length. There will be parts that bulge and stick out. Builders refer to the part that sticks out most as the high spot. You must begin by finding this high spot. You do this with a long vertical batten which you hold close to the wall, and move along its entire length. This will point out clearly where the high spot lies. A plumb line and bob can perform the same function.

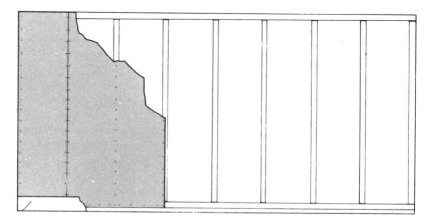

Figure 38   Cladding a brick wall with plasterboard

When you have found the high spot, hold your vertical batten on it, and use a spirit level to ensure that it is truly vertical. Make a pencil mark on the floor where the batten touches it, on the side nearest the wall, and make a corresponding pencil mark at the top on the ceiling. You now need a long true batten. Place it on the floor, its inner face on the pencil mark, and position it carefully so that it is parallel to the wall. Now draw a pencil line on the floor, along the side of the batten furthest from the wall. You will probably find it easier to do all this with accuracy if you have a helper.

A continuous, horizontal batten should now be screwed to the wall, 25 mm (1 in) up from the floor, and it should align with the pencil line on the floor. To ensure that it does this, you will have here and there to put packing (scraps of card, hardboard or timber) behind it to prevent you from screwing it hard against the wall, and thus following its contours.

Repeat the process at the top of the wall, near the ceiling, fixing another long continuous batten, aligned with the pencil line on the ceiling. Use a vertical batten, in conjunction with a spirit level, to ensure that the face of the ceiling batten is plumb with that near the floor.

In addition to these two horizontal supports, vertical ones are needed – at the edge of every board, and at 400 mm centres for the 9.5 mm thick board, or at 600 mm centres for the 12.7 mm material. Screw these battens to the wall making sure they are truly vertical, and that they are in plane with the horizontal battens at floor and ceiling level, packing out as needed.

If you know that you will be fixing heavy items here later on, fit additional battens to the wall in just the right place to receive the fixing screws of such items, which will pass through the plaster-board and into the timber behind. Should you later on find you want to fix something to a section of the wall where you have not made such provision, drill right through the board and into the wall behind, inserting your plug into the masonry.

Once the framework is completed, fix the plasterboard in exactly the same way as for a non-load-bearing partition.

For further information on plasterboard contact British Gypsum, Reddington House, Loughton Road, Reddington, Nottingham NG11.

The joinery

Once the wall is finished and the joints filled, you can tackle the joinery. At doorways, you will need a plate to cover the end of the boards and studs, and this should be of 25 mm (1 in) thick material. You may have to plane it to the correct width. Then fit door stops, which could be of 38 mm ($1\frac{1}{2}$ in) by 32 mm ($1\frac{1}{4}$ in) timber, and finally the architrave. This you buy as such from a woodyard. A number of different mouldings are available. The whole thing is shown in plan in Figure 39. The top of the door opening should be treated in the same way. A small access door to the water tank and pipes would be constructed in a similar manner.

All round the room you will need skirting board, which again is

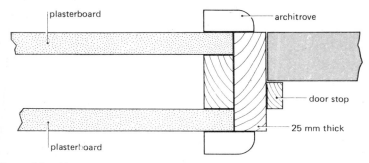

Figure 39　The joinery of a doorway

bought as a special moulding. All of these timbers can be fixed with nails or screws.

Window frames will, in the case of dormers, have been taken care of by the builders.

Decorating

Once the filler on the joints and corners has dried, you can start to decorate the plasterboard. In fact, the sooner you do so the better. If you propose to use wallpaper, then you should first seal the surface with a wallboard primer. Otherwise, you would find it extremely difficult to remove the paper when you next want to redecorate. Emulsion paint can, however, be applied without a primer.

As for the timber, treat knots with knotting, then apply a wood primer, followed by an undercoat, and one or two top coats.

Insulation

If you are using ordinary plasterboard, and need to add some form of insulation, the best material to use is 100 mm (4 in) thick glass fibre or mineral wool in blanket form. When using this on the ceiling you can drape it over the joists before you fix the plasterboard to it. Should the size of your room allow it, the blanket can cover the ceiling then drop down the wall at the far ends – buy blanket of a length to allow you to cover the whole span of the ceiling plus the walls at each end in one continuous roll. The blanket covering the walls should be well tucked into the spars of the framework.

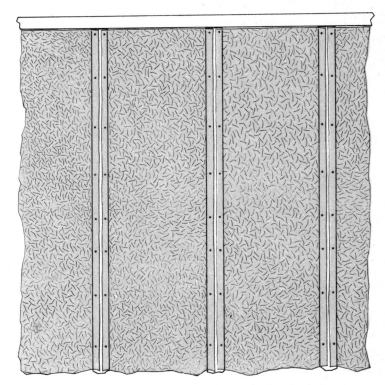

Figure 40   Insulation blanket nailed in place by its plastic overlay

   Where the walls must be insulated separately, the top of the roll needs to be securely fixed with nails at the top of the wall, and then once again well tucked in between the uprights. You could, if you wish, run tape or string horizontally and fixed to the uprights at the foot of the wall and half way up, to hold the blanket securely in place. However, it is possible to buy blanket bonded to a clear plastic, which overlaps it at the side. You fix the blanket in place by nailing through this plastic and into the studs of the wall from the inside, before the plasterboard is in place (Figure 40).

The Electrics

No matter how rudimentary your loft conversion, it is a good idea to lay on to it a supply of electricity. After all, even a gathering ground for junk is better if you can see your way around it by electric light instead of having to grope about in the dark with a torch. And, of course, if you have a full-scale habitable conversion, you will need a proper electric system.

Installation of this is definitely one of the jobs you can do yourself. No great skills of craftsmanship are involved, and in this chapter I will tell you exactly what you have to do. You might care to read it in conjunction with another book that goes into the subject more fully, and here I recommend *The Householder's Electrical Guide* by Geoffrey Burdett (Stanley Paul, £2.95).

But I must sound a warning. A mistake in electricity can have serious, if not fatal, consequences. So unless you are absolutely certain what you are doing, do not attempt this work; call in a contractor instead. One other point. I am assuming that your existing electrical installation is a modern one – i.e. that it has been installed, say, within the last thirty years. As an indication, look at the socket outlets. Square or rectangular ones, with rectangular holes for the plug pins, indicate a modern system. Circular ones, with round pin holes, mean the system is an old one. Look, too, at the light switches and roses to see if they are modern. If your system seems out of date, then it should be modernized immediately by a qualified electrical contractor – this is a much more important priority than having an extension in your loft.

All the instructions in this chapter comply fully with the *Regulations for the Electrical Equipment of Buildings* published by the Institution of Electrical Engineers, and known as the *IEE Regulations* for short. It is to these I refer when I use the phrase 'the regulations'. Unlike the Building Regulations and the planning rules, these do not have the force of law. Nevertheless, it is absolutely essential, for safety reasons, that you stick to them. But, more than that, many local authority Building Control Officers insist that you follow these regulations; many lending authorities will not advance a loan to pay for the conversion unless you adhere to them; and the local electricity board is empowered by statute not to supply electricity to an installation that flouts them from the safety aspect. So, let us move on to what you have to do to get electricity in your loft.

The theory

Electricity is taken round British homes to the points where it is needed by a series of circuits, of which there are three distinct types:

1) Lighting circuits, which, as the name implies, supply electricity to the fixed lights at the ceiling roses, or on the walls.
2) Ring circuits, which feed what are commonly known as the power points (but should more correctly be termed socket outlets) into which you plug the wide range of portable appliances in use in modern homes. Appliances up to a rating of 3 kilowatts can be plugged into a socket outlet. This includes table lamps, so a ring also forms part of a home's lighting scheme.
3) Individual circuits for larger pieces of equipment (i.e. those with a rating of more than 3 kilowatts) that are too powerful to be plugged into a socket outlet. Examples of these are cookers, water heaters, electrically operated showers, etc.

You will certainly need lighting and ring circuits in your extension. Whether, in addition, you have to install one or more of the third kind obviously depends on the use to which you wish to put your extension.

You may think of the lighting and socket outlets as being part of the finishing touches of your conversion, but in fact right from the start you must see the electrics as an integral part of your planning. In a good installation, the cables that make up the various circuits are hidden out of sight. When you are building a room in the loft from scratch, there will be no problem about this, since they can, for instance, go under the floor before it is installed, or behind the walls whilst you actually build them. So it could well be that, to take an example, running the ring circuit cable over the ceiling of your present top storey would be among the first jobs you tackle.

However, no matter what work you do initially you should always leave the final connection to the mains until the installation of the circuit is complete. This point is one that cannot be stressed too strongly. The reason for it is, of course, obvious. If you make the connection first, and then go on to work on your installation, you will inevitably touch live wires, and that could kill or maim you, if it did not start a serious fire first. So every part of a circuit should be complete before it is joined to the mains.

Following from this is the other serious safety point that whenever you are working on an electrical system, you must always shut off the supply at the mains first. So before you ever touch an electrical cable or fitting, you must always ask yourself: did I switch off?

But before we go into installation, we must first have a look at how domestic electrical systems in Britain operate. Electricity comes from the generating station into your home via a cable that ends up at what is known as the service terminal box. This has a fuse that protects your installation and allows the board's engineers to shut off the electricity supply when maintenance work is needed. The electricity supply then passes on to the meter (or meters).

Up to, and including, the meter, the installation is the property and responsibility of the board, and you must not tamper with it. Beyond the meter, the system is, in the jargon of the trade, the consumer's installation, and you may work on this.

At the heart of the consumer's installation is a metal or plastic box known as the consumer unit, which houses the mains switch and the fuses. The various circuits radiate from these fuses, and the switch allows you to shut off the electricity supply when you want to work on the system, or when you are going away from home.

The fuses are fixed into small plastic holders, called, not unnaturally, fuse holders, and these clip into what are known as fuseways. The rating of the fuse varies according to the type of circuit it will be supplying, and in modern installations there are small coloured dots on the outside of the holder to tell you the rating of the fuse. This is the colour coding:

white	5 amp
blue	15 amp
yellow	20 amp
red	30 amp
green	45 amp

It is extremely dangerous to connect a circuit to a fuse of too high a rating, because a dangerous fault might develop before the fuse blew. If you connect it to a fuse of too low a rating it might blow as soon as you switch on the electricity.

Most fuses in British homes are of what is known as the rewireable kind – i.e. a loop of wire is threaded through the holder. However, in some very modern installations the fuseways are designed to take cartridge fuses, similar in appearance to, but not interchangeable with, the fuses used in ring circuit plugs.

The cable that in modern systems carries electricity around British homes is described by the trade as being 'flat PVC sheathed and insulated, two core and earth'. Perhaps it is worthwhile elaborating a little on what that means. The fact that the cable is flat is stressed because some types of cable, used for other purposes, are circular. The phrase PVC sheathed refers to the outer covering and attention is drawn to that because other types of covering are possible – at one time domestic wiring cables were rubber and/or fabric covered, and a different type of sheathing is used for cable out of doors. The two-core part of the description refers to the two wires that carry the current – the conductors, as they are properly called. These are, of course, insulated, the live one in red PVC and the neutral one in black. No, I have not made a mistake there. The colour coding of brown for live and blue for neutral applies only to the flex of an appliance – not the cable of house wiring. There is also a third wire inside the cable – the earth, which is just a strand of bare copper. However, the regulations state that a length of green and yellow PVC sheathing, which you can buy by the metre at electrical shops, should be slipped over the end of this, to cover the whole length that is exposed, before it is connected to anything.

Cable comes in various sizes, to be used according to the type of circuit. This size is expressed in sq. mm – e.g. a lighting circuit is wired in 1 sq. mm, or sometimes 1.5 sq. mm cable, and a ring circuit in 2.5 sq. mm.

The lighting circuits

It is usual for small British homes to have two lighting circuits – one for the upstairs, and one for down, so that, if for any reason one of the circuits fails, the whole house is not plunged into darkness. Larger houses may have more circuits. Since the ring circuit would, presumably, remain live, you could in any case still get light from table lamps.

Now it may be possible for you to get enough lights in your room in the loft by extending the existing upstairs lighting circuit. But even in cases where this is allowed under the regulations (and I will shortly explain more fully what I mean by that) if you propose to have proper habitable rooms in your attic it is not a bad idea to have a separate circuit up there, once again so that if a fault throws the first-floor circuit out of action you can still have lights in your loft. Of course, this would involve you in extra work and expense, especially if there is no spare fuseway in your consumer unit – see page 115 – but would in my view be worthwhile.

If you are just using your loft for storage, then one or two lights as an extension to the first-floor circuit is a perfectly acceptable idea, provided you do not contravene the regulations in doing so.

So let's look at the regulations. They stipulate that a lighting circuit is permitted to carry a load no greater than 1200 watts. To find out the loading of a circuit, determine which are the bulbs on it, and add up the total wattage – bulbs of 100 watts or over should be taken at their face value, those under should be counted as 100 watts each.

As I said, it is highly likely that all the upstairs lights will be on one and the same circuit, and all those downstairs on another, but it is as well to check. Here's how to do that. During daylight hours, switch on all the lights in your home, noting as you do if any bulbs are not working. Replace any that are defective. Now go to the consumer unit, turn off the mains switch, and remove the fuse controlling the upstairs lighting circuit. Switch on the mains again, and note which lights are out. They are the ones on that circuit.

How do you recognize which is the correct fuse? There is usually a chart on the back of the consumer unit door telling you which is which, but if not take out the fuses in turn (remembering that, should your fuse holders be colour coded, the lighting fuses will carry a white dot). It is important, though, always to switch off before you take out a fuse. Eventually, you will come across the fuses that control the various lighting circuits.

If you were to look at the theory of house lighting as shown in diagrammatic form, it would show that the neutral wire goes directly to the light, whereas the live wire goes to it via a switch. There is, in addition, of course, the earth. When the switch is on, current passes directly to the bulb which will come alight. When the switch is off, the passage of the current is blocked, and the light cannot come on.

Two systems are in use in British homes to put this theory into effect in practice – the loop-in system, and the junction or joint-box system. The former is by far and away the most common and is the one that is always preferred in modern installations. It is the one you ought to adopt in your loft extension.

The main point in its favour is that all the connections are made – or looped-in to use the electrician's jargon (hence the name) – actually inside the ceiling rose, which has a series of terminals. The mains cable comes along to the rose and is connected to the appropriate terminals. Another length of cable will go from the rose to the switch, and this is known as the switch drop. The mains cable will pass on to the next rose in the circuit, and there may in addition be a branch line to a rose too remote to be included on the main circuit. The cable stops at the last rose on the circuit – it is not a ring, and does not return to the consumer unit. Thus it is a straight, or – to give it the proper term – a radial circuit.

The connections inside a typical loop-in circuit rose are shown in Figure 41. One point to note is that ordinary lighting cable is used for the switch drop, and this will contain a red and a black core in addition to the earth. However, both cables are in fact live, and inside the rose you will see a black cable connected to a red one – something that goes against all you have ever learned about electricity. So that you can instantly recognize this black live wire, a short length of red tape should be fixed to it at both the rose and switch ends.

How does the joint-box system differ from this? The point about it is that all the connections are made inside a joint box which will

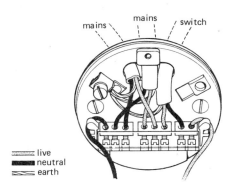

Figure 41   A typical loop-in circuit rose

be hidden out of sight somewhere – under the floor, for instance. The mains cable passes along to the box, and is connected to terminals inside it. A switch drop and lead to the rose are also wired in, and the mains cable then passes along to continue the circuit. Typical joint-box connections are shown in Figure 42. Inside the rose there will be only three wires – a live, neutral and earth. Connections at the switch are as for a loop-in system.

So now you can see why the loop-in system is preferred. All the connections are readily accessible inside the rose and the switch, so

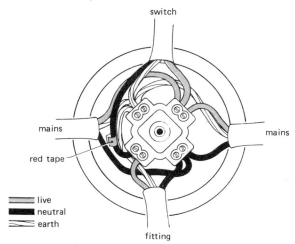

Figure 42   Joint-box lighting circuit connections

it is easy to carry out repairs should they ever become necessary. Secondly, it is much easier to extend a loop-in circuit. When you want another extra light somewhere, you merely connect up to the spare terminals inside the rose (assuming, of course, that they have not already been used for a branch line). With a joint-box system, however, you have to locate the mains cable, which will probably be hidden out of sight, and insert a box in it.

To install a lighting circuit, you must first of all plot everything out on paper. Decide exactly where you want the roses to be positioned. The exact centre of the ceiling is the usual place, but you may have other ideas – closer to a bed or dressing table in a bedroom; exactly over the table in a dining room; near the seating in a living room; and so on. Next work out the position of the switches controlling these lights. The usual practice is to site them so that they are readily accessible just inside the door.

With these two points decided, you can now plan the cable runs. The circuit should start at the consumer unit, pass along to the first rose, then the next, and so on until it reaches the last. However, it may be more economical here and there to have a branch line from one rose to a point that is remote from the rest of the run. Cable will also need to be run from each rose to its switch.

To carry out the work, install the roses and the switches, run the cable, which should be 1 sq. mm (although sometimes 1.5 sq. mm is used when a whole circuit is being installed) from a 5 amp fuseway in the consumer unit, install the switch drops, connect the cable to the terminals of the roses and switches, finally wiring up to the mains at the consumer unit. The exact way of carrying out these various tasks is detailed in the second half of this chapter.

The ring circuit

This is the circuit that takes electricity to the socket outlets. Unlike a lighting system, a ring circuit is a true ring. It is in 2.5 sq. mm cable, and starts from a 30 amp fuseway in the consumer unit, goes around the house supplying socket outlets on the way, then returns to the same fuseway. In addition to the main ring, there can be branch lines known as spurs, taking current to sockets in remote corners of the home.

There is no limit to the number of socket outlets that you can have on a ring, but the regulations do state that you must have a separate ring for every 100 sq. m (or 1000 sq. ft) of floor area of your home. (Incidentally, here do not confuse floor area with ground plan. By floor area is meant the total floor area of each of the storeys in your home.) Just as with lighting circuits, the usual practice in small British homes is to have one ring for the downstairs rooms, and another for those upstairs, even when the house is sufficiently small to be covered by one ring, so that should one circuit fail the whole house is not without power.

Now once again, it is possible that you might be able to give your room in the loft the power points you want simply by extending the upstairs ring – it would not take you long to determine if the combined floor area of your present top storey and your proposed loft extension does not exceed 100 sq. m. But once more that is probably not the wisest course. It would be far better to give your loft conversion its own ring circuit, just as it should have its own lighting circuit, so that should there at any time be anything wrong with the first-floor ring, you can still have power in the loft. There is, again, the consideration that extra expense will be involved, but I hope you will feel that it is worth it.

The ring circuit is for supplying appliances up to a rating of 3 kilowatts, which means everything from a table lamp through kitchen equipment and home entertainment items, up to and including fires or room heaters. Exactly the same type of plug is fitted to each of these different appliances, so that each and all of them can be plugged into any socket on the system. This is not a dangerous arrangement, because the fuse protecting the appliance is in the plug itself. Two sizes of fuse are used – 3 amp for appliances with a rating of up to 720 watts, and 13 amp for those between 720 and 3000 watts.

So far I have only spoken of socket outlets, but there is another type – the fused connection unit. Appliances are permanently connected to this – you cannot pull a plug out at will – and the fuse is actually inside the connection unit.

To install a ring circuit, begin by deciding just how many socket outlets you would like, and where you want them to be positioned. Since you are carrying out the installation yourself, you can be generous about this, and make sure you have enough outlets not only for your present, but also your likely future, needs. Eight in living rooms, and six in bedrooms would not be too lavish. To cut down the cost, you can install double sockets instead of singles.

Now work out on paper an economical route for the cable to take to all these outlets. If a big detour would be needed to reach the odd socket here and there, then to cut down on cable costs you can connect them up by means of a spur.

With the circuit planned, you can begin the installation. Fix the sockets in place, run the cable to them, connect it to the socket's terminals, then finally to a 30 amp fuseway in the consumer unit. In the next section I will detail exactly how these various tasks are accomplished.

Other circuits

I do not think that many people would want to install appliances such as cookers or water heaters in their lofts so, since space is limited, I will not deal with them in this chapter. If you do, however, wish to fit such an appliance you should refer to a specialist book.

The installation

In this section I will explain how to carry out the various tasks involved in installing electrical circuits. But again I must sound the warning that the consequences of a mistake in electricity can be appalling, so unless you understand thoroughly my instructions, and know what you are doing, you would do well to leave the work to an electrical contractor. And, once more, may I remind you always to switch off at the main before you touch a live circuit.

The cable

In good installations cable should be hidden out of sight wherever possible, and this should present no difficulty in your loft conversion, for you can in many cases install it as, and before, other building work goes on. Incidentally, it is customary for cable that is on view – or surface-run, to use the proper term – to be sheathed in white, but cable with grey sheathing, which is slightly cheaper, is usually specified for cable out of sight.

A very good place for hiding cable is under the floor of your room in the loft, and on top of the ceiling of what is at present the top floor. Such a spot would be ideal for most of the ring circuit cable, the cable being brought up behind the walls of the new room to be connected to the terminals of the socket outlets.

Cable running parallel to the joists can merely lie loosely on top of the ceiling below. If it has to pass across joists it should go through holes bored through their sides. Make sure that the hole is big enough to take the cable, because it might be dangerous if the insulation of the cable became chafed as it was pulled through.

So that the cable will be safe from being struck by nails or screws when you come to fix the floor – or, indeed, any nails or screws that are driven into the floor later on – the regulations say that the holes should be at least 50 mm (2 in) from the top of the joists. These holes constitute all the fixing the cable will need.

Cable can also go above the ceiling of your loft conversion and, obviously, it will be cable of the lighting circuit that is run here. It is quite likely that, when the installation of your new ceiling is complete, there will be very little space above it, so you may well decide to run this cable once the new ceiling joists are in place, but before the plasterboard is fixed. This is especially true when you remember that the wiring lies below the insulating material, which, as you will see in Chapter 6, sometimes has to be laid before the sheets of plasterboard. It is a good idea, then, to fix the cable to the ceiling joists so that it will not be disturbed during subsequent work. When you come to fix the plasterboard in place, you must take great care not to damage the cable with the fixing screws or nails.

However, if there is enough headroom above your ceiling to allow you to install the wiring after the ceiling, few fixings will be needed for cable that runs parallel to the joists because the insulation will help to keep it in place. Make sure the cable is well tucked down to the plasterboard before you lay the insulation.

Should the cable cross the joists, there is no need to go to the trouble of boring holes in the sides of the joists. Simply carry the cable over the top of the joists, fixing it to each side so that it closely hugs the timber. Plastic or buckle clips can be used for fixing the cable.

To reach the ceiling the lighting cable will have to run up the outside of the walls of your room in the loft. Once again it will not need many fixings. Cable running up or down walls to or from a socket outlet or light switch should always follow a truly vertical path so that you will know exactly where it lies in the event of your wanting to make a fixing to the wall later on.

So much for how you hide the cable once it is actually in your loft. But how does it get there? The various circuits will have to come from your consumer unit, which is almost certain to be on the ground floor of your home. It is impossible for me to give you specific advice on this point because the topography of different houses varies so much. All you can do is study the layout of your own home, and plot the best route – best being a combination of ease of installation and shortness of run, to cut down the cost of the cable. Here are some tips to help you.

There are three main ways in which cable can be hidden in a vertical run inside the house:

Buried in grooves cut in the plaster. First plot the route for the cable. As I have said, cable buried in plaster should, where possible, be truly vertical. So, using a plumb line (a length of string with a weight attached) as a guide, mark on the wall with a pencil a truly vertical line along the path you have chosen for your circuit.

With a straightedge and a knife draw a line just to the side of, and parallel to, this pencil line. Then use the knife and straight-edge to draw another line parallel to this, but the width of the cable away from it. If you intend to run two cables – say the ring and lighting circuits – up to the loft, then both can go in the same groove, providing you make it wide enough. If the wall has been papered, then first trim a strip of the paper about 25 mm (1 in) wider than the groove.

The channel – or chase, as it is called by electricians – can be cut out with an old carpentry chisel (or even a screwdriver if you wish). First run the chisel blade along the grooves made by the knife, to widen and deepen them, using a straightedge for greater accuracy. Then chop out the plaster in between the grooves down to the level of the masonry underneath, by striking the handle of the chisel with a mallet or hammer. If the resultant chase is not deep enough you will have to chop into the masonry below, this time using a cold chisel (a much tougher tool this, used by bricklayers etc., and consisting of a heavy steel blade and handle). The handle should be struck with a club hammer, again a much heavier tool than that used in carpentry.

When the chase is complete, place the cables in it, and cover them with plaster or cellulose filler. You can hold them temporarily in place, until you get around to applying the filler, with dabs of contact adhesive. Incidentally, the cable does not need any conduit or other protective covering.

One of the snags with this method is that damage is done to the decorations, so it is ideal only if you propose to redecorate soon, anyway.

Inside hollow walls. Two types of interior wall (i.e. those that do not form part of the exterior perimeter of the house) are found in the small home. The first kind are structural ones that are actually holding the house up, whilst the others are what the builder calls partitions, which are merely dividing one room off from another. Most internal walls are partitions, and many of them are hollow. They are ideal places for passing cable up from one floor to the next.

In older houses the hollow partitions will be lath and plaster walls. These consist of a series of stout vertical and horizontal lengths of timber, known as studs, to both sides of which is nailed a series of narrow laths, with thin gaps in between. These laths provided a key to hold the plaster.

Hollow walls in modern homes are usually of plasterboard, again fixed to a framework of studs, but not so many as those required for a lath and plaster wall. In rarer instances, the wall may be a factory-made partition, faced on both sides with plasterboard.

How do you locate a hollow partition? Look at the top of any internal walls when you make your preliminary inspection of the loft, and you will spot them at once.

The top will almost certainly be covered by a horizontal frame member, as will, almost assuredly, the bottom. These two members are known as plates. And there will probably be intermediate horizontal members, too. The top plate will present no problems – you simply bore a hole in it. Make it about 25 mm (1 in) in diameter, so that there will be enough room for the cable. To by-pass the intermediate members chop out a chase in the face of the wall, cutting down into the framework itself if necessary. Bore a hole in the plaster immediately above the horizontal member so that you can locate the cable to feed it into this chase, then pass it back into the void via another hole bored immediately below the stud (Figure 43).

As for the bottom plate, sometimes this will be accessible from

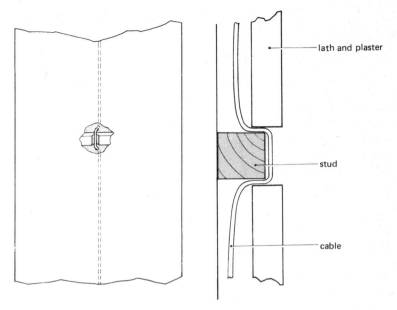

Figure 43   Feeding a cable down a lath and plaster wall

below, and you can cut a hole in it; if not treat it like an intermediate stud.

To gain access to the bottom of a partition wall, you will often have to prise up floorboards. Most floors consist of tongued and grooved boards nailed to the joists below. To take up a board, you must first cut off, with a narrow-bladed saw, the tongue on each side – the board's own tongue and that of the neighbouring board that locates in its groove. Take care during this sawing that you do not strike any electric cables or plumbing pipes below. If you want to take up only part of the length of a board, you must saw across it, just to the side of a joist. Prise up the board with an old stout screwdriver, or carpentry chisel. When you come to fix the board back in place, screw a batten to the side of the joist, and nail the board to that (Figure 44).

To reach a partition wall, the cable may have to pass up through a ceiling. Where this is so, bore a hole in the plaster using carpentry tools, and pass the cable through it.

Inside the cavity walls of the house. The external walls of most houses built in, say, the past fifty years are not solid. They consist of two separate walls – known technically as 'leaves' – with a gap between. Here and there small pieces of metal, called 'ties', are embedded in the mortar and span the gap to hold the two leaves together. The point of this gap is to stop damp from passing from the outer to the inner leaf, and also trap air that will provide insulation. It is this gap that is filled when cavity wall insulation is installed. Provided there is no such insulation in your home, you can pass cable up the gap.

But how do you know whether your home has cavity walls or not? Once again, look at the top of the external walls when making an inspection in the loft. You will see at a glance whether there is a gap or not.

When you are taking a circuit to the loft, your cable will probably just emerge through the top of the cavity. To feed it into the cavity lower down, make a hole in the wall either by boring with a drill and large-diameter masonry bit, or chopping out with a cold chisel and club hammer. You may, in some cases, have to make a similar hole near the top of the wall, for the cable to emerge from. In making the holes, avoid at all costs letting any dust drop down into the cavity, for it might lodge to form a bridge over which damp can pass to the inner leaf. As the cable is fed in, you might strike one of the wall ties, but it should be possible to avoid them.

The cable should be fixed near the points where it enters and leaves the cavity. In addition the regulations state that where a vertical drop is more than 4.6 metres (15 ft) it must have an

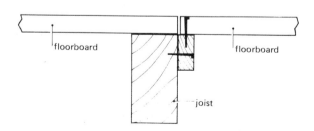

Figure 44   Fixing a floorboard back in place

intermediate fixing. The way to do that is to take the cable out of the cavity via a hole under the first-floor boards, secure it to a joist, then feed it back via another hole.

Under a floor. If the layout of your house means that a short section of the cable's run on its way to the loft must be horizontal, then the best place to hide it is under the floor. To do this you have to prise up the floorboards. For methods of fixing cable under the floor, refer back to my remarks on installing cable in the loft itself.

Running cable. When you are installing cable in a loft extension, running cable should present no problem for you can do so much of the work whilst the room is still in a skeleton state. However, you might at some time have to run the cable in confined spaces in the loft, and you will almost certainly have to do so with that length that goes through the existing part of the house. Here's what you do.

When running cable vertically, you will find that it does not necessarily drop down naturally into place under its own weight, especially in a confined space. To get over this, in the jargon of the electrician you 'drop a mouse'. A 'mouse' is a small weight – any object provided it is heavy enough, yet not too big – tied to the end of a length of string. Let us imagine you are running the cable down the middle of a cavity wall. You take hold of the string at the top of the wall, and let the mouse drop down the cavity, feeding the string gradually until the mouse reaches the desired spot – probably a hole you have cut in the wall. Now tie the loose end of the string to the cable, go downstairs, take hold of the mouse where it emerges and pull the string, which will draw the cable with it (Figure 45). Or you can work the other way if it suits your purpose – i.e. tie the string to the cable at the bottom of the drop, and pull the cable upwards.

If you want to move cable horizontally – under floorboards, or in a confined space over a ceiling, for instance – you do not even have gravity to help you. In this case, you tie the cable into a loop and feed it into one end of the run. At the other end, you insert a piece of stout wire, the end of which has been bent to form a hook. You then push this wire along until the hook engages in the loop of the cable, and you can draw the cable back towards you (Figure 46). Electricians describe this process as 'fishing for cable'. It is possible to 'fish' across fairly long distances.

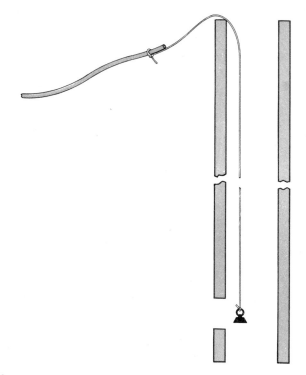

Figure 45   Running a cable down a cavity wall

Fitting a mounting box

The switches of a lighting system and the socket outlets of a ring circuit consist of two parts. To start with, there is the faceplate (the bit you see on the surface). Behind is a mounting box. This box performs two functions. Firstly, whenever the exposed ends of a set of cables are joined up to terminals, as they are behind a switch or socket, they must be surrounded by a non-combustible enclosure. The box provides such an enclosure. Secondly, the box contains threaded lugs to take the fixing screws of the faceplate – 'screws' are what the electrician calls them, although the average layman would think of them as bolts. Screws for driving into wood, the electrician describes as 'woodscrews'.

Some boxes stick out from the wall, and these are said to be surface-mounted. They are usually in white plastic. In other instances, the box is hidden below the surface, with only the faceplate on view. Such boxes are described as being flush-mounted, and are of metal. Both boxes have small round weak parts, known as 'push-outs' or 'knock-outs', precisely because you push them out to form a hole through which the cable can enter. A rubber or plastic grommet should be fixed to the hole of a metal box to stop it from chafing the cable.

There is no doubt that flush-mounted boxes are the best. Not only do they look neater, but also they are safer because you are less likely to cause damage by bumping into them. And since the walls in your loft extension will almost in every case be of hollow partitions faced with plasterboard, fitting flush-mounted boxes will be no problem. All you do is cut a hole of the right size in the plasterboard facing, insert the box and fix it by means of special fixing flanges that clamp on to the sides.

You may make use of an existing brick wall of the house for one

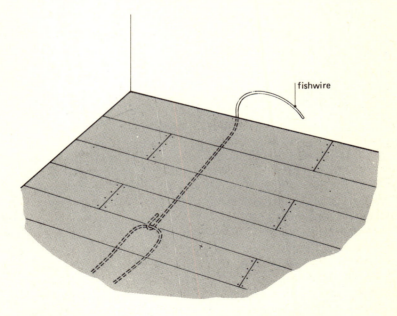

Figure 46   Running a cable horizontally under floorboards

of the walls in your extension. Since, however, you will almost certainly be cladding this with plasterboard in the manner described in Chapter 6, such a wall will present no problem. There are two methods in which a box can be fixed to such a wall. In the first place, you can use fixing flanges, just as though it were a hollow partition. Secondly, fix it to the solid wall at the back. The best way of doing this is to fix scrap wood to the solid wall before the plasterboard is in position, then drive a couple of woodscrews through holes in the back of the box, and into this scrap timber, which should be of a thickness to ensure that the box comes level, or almost so, with the face of the plasterboard.

Should you be having a solid wall professionally plastered, then it is easiest if you keep all electrical installations off this wall. Where this is not possible, however, carry out the wiring before the plasterer arrives, to save yourself the trouble of cutting out a chase for the cable. You will, however, have to run the cable in conduits, to protect it during the plastering. Boxes, too, should be installed before the plastering. If they are for light switches then they can be fixed to the surface of the wall, for the plaster can be applied in sufficient depth to come level with them. Boxes for socket outlets will need a shallow hole cutting in the brickwork with a cold chisel and club hammer.

Whatever method of fixing you use, do make sure that the box is truly horizontal, otherwise the faceplate, too, will look out of alignment when you come to screw it in place.

Boxes come in three main sizes, and in five depths. First, the sizes. For single socket outlets, you use a one-gang box, whilst a two-gang is required for a double socket outlet. The third type looks very similar to the two-gang, but it is slightly bigger, and has additional threaded lugs, so that you can fit two items to it – say a single socket, and a fused connection unit, or two fused connection units. This type is called the dual box, and it is vital that you do not confuse it with a two-gang box. Where you want two light switches side by side, use a dual-switch faceplate with a one-gang box.

Boxes are usually 25 or 35 mm (1 or 1½ in) deep. The former will do for most socket outlets, although some require the 35 mm box. For a light switch a 16 mm (⅝ in) deep special box having one adjustable lug is used. The metal version is termed a plaster-depth box for obvious reasons; the plastic-surface version is termed a shallow box. There are also specially deep boxes – 46 mm (1¾ in) in the one-gang and 47 mm for the two-gang size. These can some-times be handy for fitting in the extra cable when you want to run a spur from a socket outlet.

Installing a spur

If one of the sockets you plan is at the other end of your extension, and to take the ring there would involve a long run of cable, it could be more economical to connect up the socket by means of a spur instead. However, the regulations state that there may be only a maximum of two sockets on one spur, a double socket counting as two. But you can have as many spurs as there are sockets on the ring, once more a double counting as two.

The socket(s) on a spur are installed in the normal way, and then the length of cable feeding them has to be connected up to the main ring. There are two possible places for doing this in your loft extension. The best is undoubtedly at a socket that is on the ring itself. The wires of the spur cable are inserted into the same terminals of this socket as those of the main circuit. This is such an easy method when you are installing a ring from scratch that the alternative method should be used only when there is no ring socket remotely near the site you have chosen for those on the spur.

And what is the alternative? It is to use a joint box, which you insert in the ring circuit. The joint box should be a three-terminal one, and is mounted on a length of 75×25 mm (3×1 in) timber fixed between two joists, about 75 mm (3 in) from their top edge. This timber is supported on, and screwed to, two short bearers nailed to the sides of the joist. The red wires of all three cables – two of the ring itself, plus one of the spur – are connected to one of the outer terminals of the joint box; the three black wires are connected to the other outer terminal; whilst the three bare wires – the earth – go to the middle terminal, a length of green and yellow PVC sleeving having been slipped on the bare ends (Figure 47). Finally screw down the joint box cover.

Connecting up socket outlets

The terminals of a socket outlet are on the back of the faceplate, and there is only one set of these, no matter whether the outlet is a

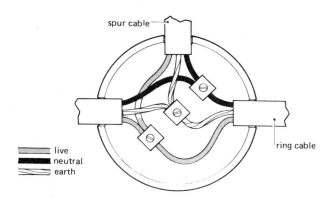

spur cable

ring cable

live
neutral
earth

Figure 47   A joint-box inserted in the ring circuit to supply a spur

double or single. The cable will come to these terminals via the holes in the mounting box screwed to the wall. Draw it through these holes, cut it to length, and strip the ends. Then the core wires of the cable can be connected to the terminals, of which there are three. The red core goes to the L (or live) terminal, the black one to the N (or neutral) terminal, and the bare wire to the E (for earth) terminal, a length of green and yellow sleeving having first been slipped over its exposed portion.

Sockets on the main ring will be fed by two cables – one coming from the previous socket on the ring, the other passing on to the next. Should the cable for a spur join the ring at this socket, there will be three cables. All the exposed cores being solid should be inserted side by side in the terminal hole, red going with red, black with black, and earth with earth. Sockets at the end of a spur will have only one cable. The bared end of the cores of this should be bent back to make sure there will be a good connection at the terminal.

Extending a ring

As I said earlier in the chapter, it is possible to install socket outlets in your loft by extending the ring of what is your present top storey. Although not such a satisfactory method, you might decide to adopt it if, for one reason or another, you feel you do not require many sockets in your new room. Of course, if you are not using your loft for habitable purposes, but merely putting it to storage or hobby use, then one or two sockets as an extension to an existing ring is a perfectly reasonable proposition.

The easiest way to extend a ring is to run a series of spurs from it. But remember the regulations about spurs? Although you can have as many spurs as there are sockets on the ring, you may have only two sockets on each spur, one double counting as two. So if you decide on a double socket in some part of your loft, install it in the normal way, and connect it as spur to a socket in a room below. Two single sockets could be treated in the same way.

There is, however, a snag. That socket in the room below might itself be on a spur, and you break the regulations if you add another socket to it. How do you tell if it is on a ring or not? You need a 9-volt battery and bulb tester, as in Figure 48. Switch off at the main, remove the faceplate, and see how many sets of cables are connected to the terminals. If there are two, the socket is either on a ring, or the first one of two on a spur. Remove the two red wires from their terminals, connect one red wire to one lead of the tester, and the second red wire to the other lead. If the bulb lights the socket is part of a ring, and you may run a spur from it. If the bulb does not light, the socket is the first of two on a spur, and you must not use it.

Should you find when you remove the faceplate that the socket

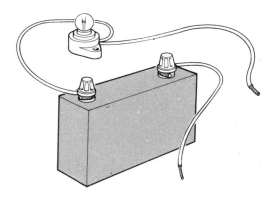

Figure 48   A 9-volt battery and bulb tester

has only one set of wires, then you know it is at the end of a spur, and you may not connect either one double or two singles to it. If it is the only one on that spur, you could connect one single to it. How do you tell? Look around in both that room and even the one next door for a socket that might, because of its position, be on the same spur. Switch off at the main, and remove its faceplate. If it has two cables, look for one going in the direction of the first socket. Connect the red and black wires of this cable to the bulb tester. Go back to the first socket and connect its red and black wires together. If the bulb does not light, the two sockets are not on the same spur. Reconnect all wires properly before restoring the power.

Connecting up wall switches

The terminals of a light switch, too, are on the back of the face-plate. A single one-way switch has two terminals, but each of the two switches of a dual switch has three – marked Common, L1 and L2. The earth terminal is not on the faceplate, but on the mounting box. For the three-terminal switch the red wire is connected to the Common and the black to the L2, the earth core going to the E terminal on the box, after a length of green and yellow sleeving has been slipped over its exposed end. Thus one terminal – L1 – is left blank. It is, in fact, used only in two-way switching (see page 113).

Since you will be using ordinary lighting cable, the cable will have a red and black core, as well as the earth, although both are, in fact, live (see page 95). Because of this, it is a requirement of the regulations that you fix a short length of red insulation tape over the insulation of the black core.

Fitting a ceiling rose

A ceiling rose performs a function similar to that of the box behind a socket outlet and switch, in that it constitutes a non-combustible chamber in which the bared ends of the circuit cable and light flex can be connected to terminals. But more than that, it usually has to carry the weight of the light fitting – which can be considerable – and so it must be firmly held in place.

The best place for fixing the rose is directly under a ceiling joist.

You may well have installed the cable of the lighting circuit in place before fixing the sheets of plasterboard that make up the ceiling. If so, when you come to fix a board at the point you have chosen for the rose, make a hole in it and feed the ends of the cables through. You can fix the rose immediately, or later when the ceiling is complete, for the wires will show you exactly where the joist is.

To fix the rose, first unscrew its cover. In the base you will see holes to take two woodscrews, and also a hole through which the cable is fed. Some or all of these holes may be push-outs. Hold the rose up near the ceiling, and draw the cable through. Then fix it in place by pushing 38 mm (1½ in) woodscrews in the appropriate holes, and driving them home through the plasterboard, and into the joist beyond.

The connections at a loop-in circuit rose are as in Figure 41 (page 96)

Two-way switching

On the staircase to, and any landing of, your new extension you will need two-way switching – i.e. the light for the staircase should be capable of being controlled by a switch both at the top and bottom of the stairs.

To accomplish this, you must fit two-way switches. One of these is connected directly to the light with the normal house-wiring cable. Now between the two switches you run a special cable. The cable is 1.0 or 1.5 sq. mm and it is three core and earth – the three insulated wires being covered in red, yellow and blue. The cable is, of course, PVC-sheathed. The cable is connected to the two light switches as shown in Figure 49.

Connecting to the mains

Your new circuits will be connected to the mains at the fuseways of the consumer unit. Before you make the connections you must of course, switch off the main and not restore power until the work is complete. A consumer unit can have any number of fuseways from two to ten, and it is good practice when an electrical system is first installed in a house to specify a unit with sufficient fuseways to leave two spare. Thus if the system first consists of two lighting and

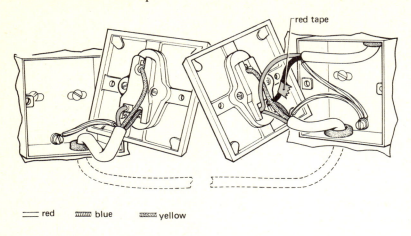

red tape

══ red   𝕞𝕞𝕞 blue   ▦▦▦ yellow

Figure 49   Connections for two-way switches

two ring circuits, a six-fuseway consumer unit may well have been installed. Should the system have included in the first place a cooker, and, say an immersion heater, as well as the lighting and ring circuits, then an eight-fuseway consumer unit should be there. And so on. Of course, it could well be that the spare units have already been taken up with extensions to the original system, and later in this chapter I will tell you what to do about that.

Fuseholders are interchangeable, so that a consumer unit can be made up from a selection of fuseholders of whatever rating you choose. But the fuses themselves are not interchangeable, which means that, for instance, a 30 amp fuse cannot be inserted in a 5 amp fuseholder.

Inside a consumer unit, as well as the fuseways, you will see a separate strip of neutral terminals, and a strip of earth terminals. To wire up a cable, its red core goes to the fuse terminal, its black one to the neutral terminal strip, and its earth to the earth strip once a length of green and yellow PVC sleeving has been slipped over its exposed end.

Since a ring circuit starts at the fuse unit, and comes back to it after passing round the house, each end of its cores is connected to the same terminal. It should be wired to a 30 amp fuseway. A lighting circuit is not a ring, thus only one end of the cores is connected to the terminals. This should be connected to a 5 amp fuseway (Figure 50).

Now let's go back to the problem that will face you if you find there is no spare fuseway in the consumer unit. The way out is to install a new mainswitch and fuse unit – known to electricians as a switchfuse unit. This is fixed to the wall, near the consumer unit and meter – preferably between the two.

The cable of your new circuit is fed in and connected to the terminals marked load – the red wire to the L terminal, the black to the N and the earth wire to the E terminal.

The switchfuse unit is connected up to the mains with special cable – 16 sq. mm single core PVC-sheathed. You need two lengths – one with red insulation, the other with black. As well as the insulation, this cable also has an outer sheathing. This may be the same colour as the insulation, or it may be grey. One end of these cables is connected to the feed terminals of the switchfuse unit – red to L and black to N. The other end is for connecting to the meter. But this is a job that must be done by the electricity board. You are definitely not allowed to do this yourself.

The board might insist on the installation of what is known as a multi-way service connector box. Into this will go the leads from switchfuse and consumer units, and out of it run the final cables to

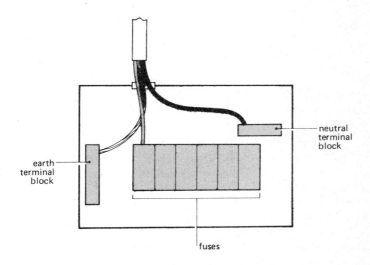

Figure 50   Connections at the consumer unit

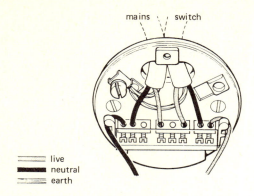

Figure 51   Installing a ceiling rose for a lampholder on a
loop-in system

the meter. Sometimes boards make a charge for this, sometimes
not.

Your switchfuse unit needs to be properly earthed. You do this
with a length of 6 sq. mm green and yellow PVC insulated earth
cable. This earth cable comes with the insulation already on – you
do not buy sleeving and slip it over bare wire. The cable is run
from the earth terminal of the switchfuse unit to the earthing
terminal of the whole installation. If you cannot find this, the earth
terminal of the consumer unit will do instead.

A light in the loft

If you are not doing a full-scale conversion, and want a light in the
attic merely to allow yourself to see clearly when you have hauled
yourself up via a loft ladder, then obviously your wiring project
will be a much simpler one.

On a loop-in system, begin by installing a ceiling rose to which a
lampholder for the bulb can be fixed. Next fix a switch, preferably
near the entrance to the loft. Run cable between the two,
connecting to the switch as already described, and to the lampholder as in Figure 51.

Look for an existing rose, run cable from the lampholder to this,
switch off at the mains, and connect up to the existing rose. The
connections are as in Figure 52.

If there is no rose nearby, or if you have a joint-box system, then
this extension to your lighting system will have to be on the

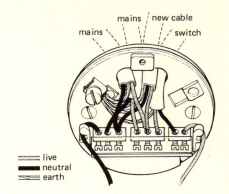

Figure 52   Connecting a new cable to an existing ceiling rose

joint-box principle.

Find the main lighting cable, which will in any event run in the loft to feed the lights of the rooms just below. In the cable install a four-terminal junction box, and connect it as shown in Figure 42 (page 96).

Useful Addresses

(mentioned in the text)

Information Centre,
Royal Institution of Chartered Surveyors,
12 Great George Street,
Parliament Square,
London SW1P 3AD
(Telephone: 01 222 7000)

Royal Institute of British Architects,
66 Portland Place,
London W1N 4AD
(Telephone: 01 580 5533)

National Home Enlargement Bureau,
PO Box 67,
High Wycombe,
Bucks. HP15 6XP
(Telephone: High Wycombe 711649)

Velux Co. Ltd,
Telford Road,
Eastfield Industrial Estate,
Glenrothes,
Fife KY7 4NX
(Telephone: Glenrothes 772211)

Magnet & Southern Ltd,
Royd Ings Avenue,
Keighley,
West Yorkshire BD21 4BY
(Telephone: Keighley 61133)

Chipboard Promotion Association Ltd,
7a Church Street,
Esher,
Surrey KT10 8QS
(Telephone: Esher 66468/9)

British Gypsum,
Reddington House,
Loughton Road,
Reddington,
Nottingham NG11
(Telephone: Nottingham 844844)

Index